T0129826

God's Gift to You

A Sequel

Fred Ithurburn

Order this book online at www.trafford.com
or email orders@trafford.com

Most Trafford titles are also available at major online book retailers.

Printed in Victoria, BC, Canada.

ISBN: 978-1-4269-1666-3 (soft)
ISBN: 978-1-4269-1667-0 (hard)

Library of Congress Control Number: 2009934822

Our mission is to efficiently provide the world's finest, most comprehensive book publishing service, enabling every author to experience success. To find out how to publish your book, your way, and have it available worldwide, visit us online at www.trafford.com

Trafford rev. 11/25/2009

 www.trafford.com

North America & international
toll-free: 1 888 232 4444 (USA & Canada)
phone: 250 383 6864 ♦ fax: 812 355 4082

INTRODUCTION

Ever since my Roman Catholic Church authorized me, as a lay person and an extraordinary Eucharistic minister, I take Communion to the sick who are unable to come to Church for our Eucharistic sacrifice. With recipients, I have prayed the following prayer:

> **God Our Father,**
>
> **You have called us to share the one bread and to become one in Christ. Help us to live in him that we may bear fruit. Rejoicing that he has redeemed the world. Amen.**

The appropriateness of the prayer's use obviously comes from its all-inclusive Eucharist. But, my Church's objection to the unworthiness of many has persuaded me to write an argument for the many excluded peoples of the world. Our Lord's way, the Roman Catholic Church's way, and the Church of Christ's way— each way calls for the Eucharist to be free for everyone, as I argue hereafter.

1. OUR LORD'S WAY

Our Roman Catholic Church's *Eucharist Prayer* repeats Jesus' essential words at the Lord's Supper, and it keeps intact the words the Lord expressed at the Last Supper. We continue that prayer in every Mass to date, as follows:

> Before he was given up to death, a death he freely accepted, he took bread and gave you thanks. He broke the bread, gave it to his disciples, and said:
>
> **Take this, all of you, and eat it:**
>
> **This is my body which will be given up for you.**
>
> When supper was ended, he took the cup. Again he gave you thanks and praise, gave the cup to his disciples, and said:
>
> **Take this, all of you, and drink from it:**
>
> *This is the cup of my blood, the blood of the new and everlasting covenant. It will be shed for you and for all so that sins may be forgiven.* **Do this in memory of me.** (Italics mine)

Catholics, at Mass, overhear the phrase, "this is the cup of my blood, the blood of the ***new and everlasting covenant.*** It will be shed for you and for all so that sins may be forgiven." Most are not aware of what this "new covenant" means, nor do they appreciate what God-given rights the covenant provides for us in Christ. Jesus came to seal this *new covenant*, which truly gives light and forgiveness of sins. A covenant is a solemn agreement between God and his people which, in this one's case, also establishes a new kingdom and relationship between humanity and God. St. Paul was the first to use the verb "Eucharist" to refer to the thanksgiving memorial banquet that Jesus Christ instituted at his Last Supper for us to thank God for Covenant and Eucharist.

These words of Jesus give meaning to the sacrificial death that He endures to establish the New Covenant and Eucharist.

God spells out his New Covenant pledges in chapter 31, verses 31 to 34 of The Prophecy of Jeremiah (Douay Version), as follows:

The New Covenant

31. Behold the days shall come, saith the Lord, and I will make a new covenant with the house of Israel, and with the house of Juda: 32. not according to the covenant which I made with their fathers, in the day that I took them by the hand to bring them out of the land of Egypt: the covenant which they made void, and I had dominion over them, saith the Lord. 33. But this shall be the covenant that I will make with the house of Israel, after those days, saith the Lord: I will give my law in their bowels, and I will write it in their heart, and I will be their God, and they shall be my people. 34. And **they shall teach no more every man his neighbor, and every man his brother, saying: Know the Lord, for all shall know me from the least of them even to the greatest, saith the Lord: for I will forgive their iniquity, and I will remember their sin no more.**

Four hundred years later, God was pleased to bring his people together as one in Jesus Christ. Our Lord's way of preparation was done, and as a figure of that new and perfect covenant, Jesus Christ ratified and fulfilled it. As the risen Jesus Christ, He again fully revealed it in His dramatic revelation to Paul (Saul). In turn, Paul dutifully reported the historical facts that, in Jesus' blood, God institutes the New Covenant by His sacrifice of Himself for us all, as follows:

Institution of the Eucharist

23. For I received from the Lord what I also handed on to you, that the Lord Jesus, on the night he was handed over, took bread, 24. and, after he had given thanks, broke it and said, "This is my body that is for you. Do this in remembrance of me." 25. In the same way also the cup, after supper, saying, "This cup is the *new covenant* in my blood. Do this, as often as you drink it, in remembrance of me." 26. For as often as you eat this bread and drink the cup, you proclaim the death of the Lord until he comes. (The New American Bible, 1 Cor 11:23-26) (Italics mine)

In previously edited sermons, Pope Benedict XVI learnedly preached that Jesus' words at the Last Supper were "interdependent" with his death on the cross, and he preached that they give meaning to a death that would otherwise be a meaningless execution. According to typescript of his lectures, he also taught at the University of Tübingen that Jesus did not intend to found any church but his universal Church of Christ, the foundation of which is in the words of Jesus in the Last Supper, where Jesus links the themes of the paschal Lamb (Ex 12), *new covenant* (Jer 31), and the suffering servant who gives himself up "for many" (Is 53). Also, Benedict taught the "for many" (Mk 14:24) prevents the church from becoming simply a select community of the righteous, a community that condemns the wayward masses to perdition. Our wayward Church heard another tune, however.

Some of us imagine that at Mass, time and space are arrested, the sacrifice of Calvary and Eucharist are one event, and we stand at the foot of the cross to perceive Jesus in his agony, suffering death for us. It is an act of adoration offered to God, an offering which we are stirred to join. We experience Jesus throughout the *Eucharistic Prayer*, when Christ returns to us in the sharing of our Lord's actual presence, his body and blood. We consume it in Holy Communion. The Real Presence within us transforms us as God wishes. Sadly, the Church invites few to accept this opportunity to learn God as Love.

As we consume the Real Presence of Our Lord, we proclaim Jesus' death, which saves all of us from eternal death. By the mystery of Jesus' death, Christ teaches us love, pardons us of evildoing, and saves us all for eternal life. By the blood of the *Covenant*, which Jesus sheds, He ratified and instituted the new relationship, the kingdom of God, which his death purchased. We also are freed of laws, except God's law to love God and impartially love each other. Love means to choose to do good for others, usually at your expense. The least and greatest of us will be mysteriously imprinted with knowledge of how to know God and His law of love, each in a way God deems to be proper for us. The Eucharist adds God Himself to transform us.

God pledges that the least with the greatest shall know, each in his own way, about love. Although disputed by those who contend that Jesus was always divinely conscious, He too, emptied of his divinity, learned to know more than what was probably known to an age thirty Jew of his day. He learned by experience, as we do, according to the Catechism of the Catholic Church. Because He had both a unique background and a mother who kept things in mind, He likely knew that He was destined to be the Messiah, and

He learned from scripture to be the suffering servant and mediator of the New Covenant. Thus, as He matured in knowledge, through His last breath on the cross, He realized and freely meant to die for all mankind as his Father, God, expected him to do. He also learned that we all were equal and not some "dogs" as He once said. Since He questioned if He could perform the task He was about to do, He sweated in the Garden as any man with similar doubts, reason, and disposition would do. Later, He was violently scourged, perhaps because the soldiers figured Pilate might release him, but also to avenge Peter's cutting off of another soldier's ear. Later, the piercing of the spear revealed the trauma Jesus internally sustained. It explained what disabled Him in carrying the cross alone, and it explained what shortened His life on the cross to mere hours. The hours of agonizing penetration of nails into all four extremities gave us the word excruciating to describe His pain as He was crucified. He truly must have tortured Himself in standing with his weight on the piercing nails as supports in order to avoid suffocation. Momentarily, He withstood the acute pain of the nails to draw a breath, and as He fatigued, He sank down into increasing panic and suffocation until He needed to breathe again and prevent asphyxiation. The torture of crucifixion was deliberate, so as to dissuade slaves from attempting to escape and criminals from repeating their crimes. Thus, His use of the cross as a pulpit was markedly brief, and whatever He afforded to say was an increased sacrifice and expenditure of life for us. For instance, "Forgive them for they know not what they do" took a lot out of him. He saved most for His Father, such as His cry from His native language, the opening of Psalm 22, "My God, My God, why have you abandoned me . . . ." As He died, "It's finished, into your hands I commit my spirit!" was also a precious expression of love for our benefit. He loved us to the end. Reflect on us in similar straits, speaking until we no longer can stand on nails—sinking down into suffocation and rising on nails again to breathe or speak. Each time we spend this energy on rising, we must overcome the progressive fatigue resulting from bleeding to death. Empathizing, consider that "I thirst" is a symptom of those bleeding to death, as fluids drain away. It proves Jesus' manner of death. Thereby signified is how we too would die. He gave His all for our benefit as He shed the Blood of the New Covenant out of love.

Father Raymond Brown, the Church's accepted expert on the scriptures, reported his faith conviction that Jesus Christ and St. Paul were simply wrong, as creatures of their culture, in believing in Satan (*St. Anthony Messenger*, March 1971). But, he confirms that Jesus is like us. Our *Catechism of the Catholic Church*, a product of Cardinal Ratzinger's thinking in the mid-1990s, also describes Jesus acting with a human mind, increasing in wisdom and learning with the use of his experience. Previously, Pope Pius X formally condemned the proposition that "Christ did not always have the consciousness of his messianic dignity." Today, we should be more enlightened, and we have the advantage of hindsight in knowing the world's not flat and in knowing that when Jesus died, he actually need not have worried about accomplishing his task or about God's absence. God is there all the time to love and save us, and He is there for all of us forever, whether we believe or reject the fact of God.

Today, Pope Benedict XVI claims that John's Gospel has eyewitness veracity. John's writings likely contributed to the foundation of Thomism's school of faith and reason, which indoctrinated Catholics to Christ's divine consciousness and led to Pope Benedict's opinion on John. John does not mention Jesus' thoughts of abandonment by God, but those thoughts were factual. This ignorance on the part of Jesus gave greater glory to His moral courage to persist in trust alone in God's love. It also increased the quality of love He showed for us. His faith, the faith of a Jew educated primarily in the Torah, was to believe we were destined to everlasting perdition if he gave up and did not persevere to the end of his life. Being indoctrinated in the teachings of the Old Testament, he probably assumed it was better that Judas had never been born.

However, the New Covenant that Jesus established in the Synoptic Gospels has God, through Jesus' death, forgiving everyone's iniquity and teaching us how to know God from the beginning to the end of time, simply out of His goodness. I submit that it fulfills our good news and that the world should have peace of mind because all of us are redeemed. Thus, Judas was forgiven of his iniquity on Jesus' death, and, except for the chastisement by Jesus he faced in the hereafter, Judas will be with the lot of us to enjoy sharing the divinity of Christ forever more. Therefore, Judas' birth was good, and God brings goodness out of our evildoing simply because He loves us all and lovingly uses us. Be assured God did not make any one of us in his image, recreated by Jesus' blood, so we would be separate from Him.

Jesus' "I thirst" complaint to me means that He was bleeding to death and that His fluids were leaving the body. However, to those influenced by the acceptance of Christ's constant divine consciousness, the "I thirst," may be a sign of His thirsting for the contrite whom He came to save. I strongly suggest that this sentiment, contributed to by the writings like John's human precepts, does an injustice to the human suffering that Jesus experiences. Had Jesus possessed God's knowledge throughout, the whole passion would not stir the likes of me to love him for the acting. Thomas Acquinas said a precious thing concerning the Eucharist sacrifice. He said, "Through the Passion of Christ, man knows thereby how much God loves him, and he who abides in love abides in God and God in him." So, John likely wrote out of his informed conscience, but no one corrected his opinions. Today, his opinions detour our Church in regard to its Eucharist and its New Covenant acceptance.

The people who authored the Gospel According to John depict a different Jesus in passion and dying. They ignore the

Covenant, making no mention of it, and they have Jesus washing his Apostle's feet to symbolize the service and absolution roles they were to have in the future. I can excuse, but not justify the arrogance of the writer's righteousness. John's Chapter 6 seems to be an anomaly passage with its verb of gnawing bread, as though the author(s) assumed the Eucharist existed prior to their writings on the "Bread of Life," as instituted at the Last Supper. As a result, in Christian Churches, the New Covenant still is not considered to be mentionable in anything other than name. Besides, Jesus' talk of nourishment at the Samaritan's well could imply John's idea that bread and wine consumption may be doing the will of his Father. These are endearing human sentiments, but not God's words. According to Luther, a learned Catholic theologian in his day, the non-consideration of the New Covenant has made our salvation a matter of our performance of good works or faith alone. It describes a bilateral agreement taught by mere human precepts. I submit that the exchanges on our part should instead be acknowledged on how to reduce or avoid chastisements in the hereafter, and the Catholic Church can still find meaning in the teaching and forgiving roles that are impliedly prohibited or made unneeded by the New Covenant. Arguably, mitigating chastisement secures Catholicism a mission for years to come, not concerning salvation, because God has unilaterally furnished us redemption in the Blood of the Covenant, but in the pledge that God will "remember their sin no more." Since, Jesus Christ is to judge us after death and weigh our good and bad doings, the sin that Christ is to consider is that sin determinative of our chastisement, if any—perhaps purgatory time, or reincarnating us as a snail, or whatever is planned for hereafter. Once justice has been done, God's pledge to forget our sin forever will be performed.

However, the author(s) of the Fourth Gospel depict Jesus as parroting what God tells Him to say, and as a superman untouched by human sensations of doubt and pain, He rises to

His glory while still nailed to the cross. I can empathize with faith convictions of Jesus' excruciating suffering, but I cannot identify with Jesus in the Second Person role of the Trinity described by the Fourth Gospel. My sister-in-law, a retired Sister of Charity, says, in regard to my enforced monologue, that my spiritual shepherds, both Pope Benedict and my diocesan bishop, try to obey their respective consciences in defending or withholding their faith convictions. Accepting her wisdom, the advocate in me still argues that we could say the same for the writers of The Gospel According to John, to Luther, to Judas, and to yours truly. I do question the opinions of my leaders—men like the writers of the Fourth Gospel, Saint Aquinas on knowledge of Jesus, and Augustine's argument with Pelagius on Original Sin—and I concede that we all try to obey our respective consciences in describing faith convictions. I disagree with them on the Eucharist and New Covenant subjects, and I feel our disagreements should be debated or discussed for the good of the Church. These are objective gifts from God and not to be subjectively discarded by men.

Pope John XXIII is incontestably a loveable individual of another sort. He called the Second Vatican Council by inviting bishops worldwide to freely reason and decide how to return the Church of Christ to fully and completely subsist in the Catholic Church as Jesus Christ intended and instituted through his passion and death. Pope John was instrumental in our seeking *ressourcement*, which means to study and return to what God, in Christ, intended the Church to be. God's saving action in history intended to use a universal church. Pope John also caused the Church to open Christ's teachings to the world. Thomism, the traditional Church teaching, based partly in John's writings, proved incredible to the enlightened world that makes up the Church of Christ. Because the Catholic tradition of intimate relationship between faith and reason fails to sustain credibility in the enlightened mainstream of society, we need to return to

Christ's Covenant to sustain the Church's mission. We should return the Catholic Church to subsisting in the Church of Christ. Pope Benedict XVI still futilely argues that Islam should be more reasonable, and he thinks the Church can better teach them. The task remains with us today, because people with fixed opinions can learn, but also resist teachings. Pope John XXIII died in 1963, before he could return us to the universal Eucharist and Covenant from which the world could learn.

The Second Vatican Council called for efforts of analysis to solve problems of the Church in the modern world. Its openness called Catholics, theologians, the teaching church, and the faithful to a new analysis to deal with accepting the universe as still in the process of evolving. The Council's thoughts acknowledged that people must recognize their lives as part of the ongoing creation of the world. God invites the universe to be more outwardly centered on God, who is fully incarnate in Christ. But, the Roman Catholic Church decided to do it the traditional way. In Christ's suffering and death, we are still invited and stirred into the embrace of God and to pursue our religious quest toward Him as our center and goal. But, Christianity's failure to motivate many people to fully participate in the work in progress evidences Christianity's rejection of God's proposed Covenant to teach and forgive us Himself. The universal Eucharist and the New Covenant relationship have never been tried. Yet, it is God's way to redeem the world. We must have faith and use God's Covenant.

The inner governmental body of the Catholic Church, the curia or Magisterium, was restrained in Vatican II so as to allow free discussion. The role of the curia was an issue to be decided. Unfortunately, on Pope John's death, the curia returned in power to write up the Dogmatic Constitution on the Church (*Lumen Gentium*), which Pope Paul VI promulgated in November of 1964. However, the spirit of openness from the Council had already been freed, and the idea of the global Church of Christ remains recognized by notables, such as Karl Rahner, as the best thing produced by the Council's Popes and assembled bishops. A gem of a record preserving this global concept exists in *Lumen Gentium*, in part, as follows:

> This is the one *Church of Christ* which in the Creed is professed as one, holy, catholic and apostolic, which our Savior, after His resurrection, commissioned Peter to shepherd (citation), and him and the other apostles to extend and direct with authority (citation), which he erected for all ages as "the pillar and mainstay of the truth" (citation). This Church constituted and organized in the world as a society, **subsists** *in the Catholic Church*, which is governed by the Successor of Peter and by the bishops in communion with him, although many elements of sanctification and of truth are found outside of its visible structure. These elements, as gifts belonging to the Church of Christ, are forces impelling toward catholic unity. (Italics mine)

Ironically, as young Ratzinger, Pope Benedict XVI actively witnessed the Council and wrote a book enthusiastically in support of the Church's new openness. As young Ratzinger, he wrote his doctoral dissertation on St. Augustine's confrontation with Donatism, a North African movement that denied their sacraments to wayward members. Both Ratzinger and Augustine regarded the lack of the fundamental virtue of charity in denying the sacraments as prevention of Donatism from being true Church. The true Church could not be founded on the exclusion of others, an idea apparently forgotten by an ambitious Ratzinger as he gained favor with Church traditionalists in championing exclusion of many from our Eucharist. Meanwhile, the Church selected the few righteous to be redeemed, leaving condemnation "for many" and thusly contradicting the prior teachings of Professor Ratzinger.

In about 1968/9, Catholic theologians and New Testament scholars from Vatican II criticized the Roman Catholic Church's Eucharist because of its exclusiveness, and they contended that the Eucharist continues the meals that Jesus had held (*God Is Near Us*, p. 59). This means that the Eucharist is a sinner's banquet where Jesus invites everyone without exception. It necessarily is an open table to which all may come to encounter the universal God, without any limit or denominational preconditions. From this time, Father Joseph Ratzinger opposed the Bible experts. Pre-Council traditions prevail today, even in the face of Jesus quoting Isaiah that hierarchies hypocritically tend to cling to human tradition and disregard God's commandment of impartially loving each other. Ratzinger's opposition has been successful, and theologians and New Testament scholars have been silenced as he has elevated.

I attended a funeral Mass at an Episcopal Catholic Church, and it seemed to agree with the spirit of Vatican II. Untouched by Pope Benedict's influence, the celebrant, a woman priest, invited us at the Breaking of Bread, by saying:

> *This is the table, not of the Church, but of the Lord. It is made ready for those who love him and for those who want to love him more. So come, you who have much faith and you who have little, you who have been here often and you who have not been here long, you who have tried to follow and you who have failed. Come, because it is the Lord who invites you. It is His will that those who want Him should meet Him here.*

With such an invitation, I could not resist, and I confess that I approached the Communion rail, thinking I might cross my arms. However, the familiarity of kneeling to receive the Eucharist, followed by the priest handing the host toward me, carried me in a habitual momentum to receive and consume Communion. It is unlikely that I will repeat the occasion.

In my previous publication, *God's Gift to You,* at page 51 I told a story which bears repeating here, "In an inner city church, an unkempt homeless woman and her son wandered in and stuck her supermarket basket in the aisle. They watched the Mass in wonder, then followed the others in the congregation to Communion, and held out their hands. The priest said without hesitation, 'The Body of Christ,' and they answered, quavering, 'Amen.'" Not mentioned in my book is my first take on reading the story—that Our Lord is likely ecstatic to be intimately within nonbelievers to transform their lives and faith. In view of the trust these two had, I feel guilty of hypocrisy in doubting the efficacy of the Episcopal Church's Eucharist, and I am open to discussing my prejudiced feeling.

An element of God's redeeming action in Covenant is the invitation of Christ, "Take this, *all of you,* and eat it; this is my body which will be given up for you" (Italics mine). Pope Benedict XVI previously preached that the words were "interdependent" with the world-redeeming death of Jesus, and I enjoy reminding him of this truth we agree upon. Since Jesus' death established God's pledge and forgives us our evildoing, the words instituting the Eucharist left me wondering why the Sacrament is part of God's saving action of mankind. Why add a cleansing memorial, especially when the Catholic Catechism states it is not ordered to cleanse? Perhaps an answer includes the final part of the Covenant's pledge, where the Eucharist cleanses residuals, "I will . . . remember their sin no more." The Eucharist is God's Gift and later a Church Sacrament to reconcile us of sin residuals, in addition to granting us other mysterious graces that transform our lives and faiths. We comply because Jesus simply says to "take," and the Eucharist might be Christ's other teaching instrument that God uses to imprint within us additional knowledge in company with His pledged forgiveness. Meditating on the acute sufferings of Christ being crucified for our benefit will stir those who are indifferent to learn or to love because of closed minds or hearts. Matters that cannot be taught may be learned, especially if the learners share in the Real Presence of Christ in Eucharist.

Mother Teresa said the daily Holy Communion strengthened her sisters to work the gutters of Calcutta. Whatever good it does in the sisters, I suggest that a greater purpose for Christ's Eucharist, as well as for Christ's Covenant membership, is to include the prostitutes and drugees of Calcutta with the sisters in sharing Eucharist. Many of these potential recipients neither have the luxury of choice or belief in a Covenant nor of Eucharist. These are gifts God entrusted to us. But, because we deem others unworthy of the gifts, and because their evildoing threatens to soil us and the Real Presence, we deny them God's gifts. Returning to glimpse Jesus naked on the cross and nailed to a tree that possibly has the excrement of its prior occupant should dispel our distaste at the brothel occupant or the recidivist drugee further soiling Christ. They are prized candidates to be Christ's siblings, and they are expected guests at Eucharist. Christ expressly invites them to his table. Who are we to say what God already cleaned needs Church cleansing? Christ called us hypocrites when we insisted on his guests washing hands as traditionally expected, and he pointed out we tend to cling to tradition and disregard God's commandment of love. God designed us to love ourselves, and in Christ's Blood of Covenant, He cleanses us to be One in Christ, loving like He loves.

In April 2008, Pope Benedict XVI, citing Pope John XXIII's teachings, preached to the UN General Assembly that governing bodies are all obligated to uphold human rights, and their failure to protect against such violations make governing bodies illegitimate. I contend that the denial of Eucharist to anyone by the Church is an illegitimate act. It is a God-given right of possession to every human being, bar none. The Church cannot legitimately deny this right or the freedom of religion which would allow everyone to receive Holy Communion while retaining the faith convictions they possess.

However, our exclusive attitudes and denial of basic rights intimidates most everyone not expressly invited to the Lord's Supper by the Church. They are neither aware nor appreciative of the fact that they, as human beings, have incontestable rights to be part of Christ's purchased Covenant. They are invitees of Christ's order to "Take this, all of you" in respect to the Eucharist. Furthermore, they should be informed about the rights we withhold and conceal from them. Many an invitee will reject the Eucharist because of the traditional prejudice held against them by the self-righteous, whom Jesus called "hypocrites" for insisting that his guests wash their hands. But even Pope Benedict knows the demands of the law of love, and as spiritual leader of the Roman Catholic Church, he knows that he should repeat Christ's invitation and instruct all would-be recipients of the Eucharist of their God-given rights. He has publicly expressed their incontestable freedom of conscience, and since God forgave their evildoing in the Blood of the Covenant, Pope Benedict XVI should again invite them to repent for his personal wrongdoings, stating the following:

> With the pope as the expression of the binding claim of ecclesiastical authority, there still stands one's own conscience, which must be obeyed before all

else, even against the requirement of ecclesiastical authority. This emphasis on the individual, whose conscience confronts him with a supreme and ultimate tribunal, is one in which the last resort is beyond the claim even of the official church.

"Truth!" said Pilate. "What does that mean?" According to "John," he was responding to Jesus saying that He came to testify to the truth. At the Second Vatican Council, the subjective opinions of bishops and theologians also spoke to the truth as they saw it. The U.S. bishops and those such as Father J.C. Murray, S.J. made a great contribution by speaking for us and teaching the Catholic Church about our new views of religious liberty. Pope John XXIII supported Murray concerning the U.S. proposition of "We hold these truths," which by law freed us from governmental interference. In 1998, Pope Leo XIII's encyclical condemned freedom of religion as a threat to civil societies and to true religion. The enlightening of the council by U.S. influence resulted in the spirit of democracy and freedom of thought added to their exercises of ressourcement. No one mentioned it, but an appropriate thought here would be to acknowledge that the act of ressourcement is going back to the new Covenant that Jesus so dearly established, which bypasses Leo XIII's encyclical and the Gospel According to John to attain the truths Jesus both testified to and died for. "We hold these truths to be self-evident, that all men are created equal, that they are endowed by their Creator with certain unalienable rights, that among these are life, liberty, and the pursuit of happiness." The quote is from our Declaration, and I submit that a truth and right of equality exists in our priesthood, which should allow women to consecrate the Eucharist.

Free bread and free wine may be an apparent incentive to most everyone to come to meet the Lord, but the real gift behind the scene is God Himself, simply for the taking, to intimately be within us all. Note, Pope Benedict did not have the willingness to excommunicate anyone in *Sacramentum Caritatis*, but like Pilate washing his hands of Jesus, he passed the matter onto diocesan bishops, who, if like my own, were already conditioned to blindly obey the Church's traditions or the Pope's predispositions. By promulgating statutes, my bishop denied all but the few their rights to Holy Communion and God's Presence.

Many Catholics already follow the dictates of their own conscience. For example, in face of Pope Paul VI's *Humanae Vitae*, our young married couples obviously conscientiously regulate birth control in disobedience. Yet, these many rise together at Communion time to receive the Eucharist, not in rebellion to the Church law, but in a rightful disobedience to its application in order to obey their view of a higher law of charity or conscience in Christ's teachings. They obey the reasons in conscience over less reasonable Church laws. They obey Christ's law of love over the Church's dogmas of human precepts.

Our Lord Jesus ordered that we not lord it over each other as the Gentiles do, but the likes of Constantine and Augustine influenced us to discipline ourselves to Catholic Rome's order. Augustine from Hippo advised the Church to accept the Platonic rule by elites, denying us the democracy Jesus had in mind. The Second Vatican Council, enlightened by our bishops from the USA, opened a window to illuminate the democratic thoughts of Jesus, but it was slammed shut again by successors to Pope John XXIII. Previously, Pope Pius XII foresaw a democratic future for the Catholic Church, and the modern world shows it bodes ill to continue the dark and feudal age of our monarchic Catholic Church. Modern enlightenment discredits the faith and reason of the aged Church's messianic claim to save the world, rather than commit itself to the New Covenant of God, who already saved the world from within the core culture of the world itself. St. Augustine's doctrine of Original Sin, which we supposedly inherited from Adam and Eve, influenced most Church thought. He fabricated this concept in the face of the Church scripture, ignoring our New Covenant inheritance where Christ's death forgave our evildoing. Augustine and the Church soiled what God cleansed with a made-up sin needing Church forgiveness in Baptism for the most innocent of us. The Church's uncharitable exclusiveness continues this theme of soiling everyone but Catholics, as evidenced by the *Dogmatic Constitution* (*Lumen Gentium*), a doctrine promulgated by Pope Paul XVI and thereafter supported by Pope John Paul II and Pope Benedict XVI. Plainly, it denies evidence of God's agreement, an anti-Christ denial that ignored the fact of the Covenant and its unilateral divine performance. It is a blasphemy to the Holy Spirit, and it simply negates God's design for salvation of everybody. The Lord's design was secured in God's New Covenant pledges and executed in Christ's blood. Use of the Covenant was to be strengthened by the accompaniment of the universal Eucharist.

The openness of John XXIII's ideal Church of Christ challenged the Catholic Church to join the enlightened mainstream of the world. Pope John feared that civilization based on reason had seeds of its own destruction in this nuclear age. We barely avoided it in WWII when defending against Hitler. The Church has yet to have a dialogue with this evolved society of humanity about awareness of its New Covenant relationship or about the diminished importance of academics on faith and reason. For centuries, the Gospel According to John's Greek philosophy and its scriptural or mythological theology were traditionally enshrined as Church's teachings through Augustine and Aquinas. This philosophy remains the Church's main teaching, and it is the basis for our anti-Christ failings. It is not credible in today's modern educated community, whose enlightenment naturally advanced over Greek philosophy and rejected the Bible's stories as fiction. The apparent threat of losing the integrity of the Church's mission calls for us to return to the Lord's or Christ's way rather than the Catholic Church's way.

The problem is not with the grass-root members of the Church who evolved beyond the feudal Catholic Church, as have the third world populace. I suggest that they are New Covenant residuals who escaped Catholicism, which establishes that God, in Christ, performs our evolution. However, the institution of the Roman Catholic Church refuses to see the obvious and insists on lording over Catholics with their subjective opinions and old-fashioned lessons of doing tradition as usual. The Catholic hierarchy thinks it knows better than the Lord when it comes to how the Church of Christ is to subsist in Catholicism. Thus, the Church's Eucharist excludes most of the world. People are written out of the Constitution, and the Church negates God's Covenant, denying Catholicism status of True Church while the hierarchy continues failing to see that their empire is naked. Our spiritual leaders have woefully failed to accomplish the Church's mission their way, which they do instead of conforming to Christ's way. They have never tried the New Covenant relationship with God. They feel bound by church teachings and the discipline of human traditions, "we have always done it this way." Both attitudes likely have proved self-defeating over the last two millennia.

Clearly, the New Covenant was ratified in Christ, instituted by Christ, and fulfilled in Christ's blood. It made a new relationship between God and man according to God's unilateral formation and performance of the Covenant agreement, coming simply out of His goodness and love for us. Accepting it as God intended should bring peace of mind. The kingdom that Jesus had earlier sent off His disciples in twos to announce has come, no strings attached, with His death for all God's people. This God/human relationship began at the beginning of creation, continued through Jesus' death, and is to be completely possessed by humanity forever with God in the hereafter. The problem to God's plan in Christ is the fact that the Roman Catholic Church insists on doing it the Church's way. As Peter's rock, it has proved not to be a foundation, but a blocking obstacle. It blocked a way of life that we never tried. So, it has yet to prove its worth. I must leave it to others to try it out because at my 77 plus years of age I won't be here to witness it. Trusting Our Lord, I hope to perceive its success from wherever I end up. However, Pope Benedict XVI is older than me. He and Pope John XXIII are of comparable age. But, Pope Benedict XVI has a spiritual shepherd to imitate in having us perform in the Church of Christ's way.

2. *ROMAN CATHOLIC CHURCH'S WAY*

I previously wrote *God's Gift To You* in reference to the Roman Catholic Church's Eucharist, which Jesus invited every human being to "take" at his Last Supper. Present Pope Benedict XVI twisted the invitation to deny the Eucharist to most everyone with the exception of a few Catholics who agree with him. I wrote over 200 letters to Pope Benedict to change his mind or heart, and I recorded most of them in *God's Gift To You*. Now, I write this sequel to publish letters on the same subject matter that I later wrote to him from April 2008 to April 2009. Plus, I added a concern for the good of the Church in its mission for the life of the world, a concern discovered while attempting to overcome the monologue of correspondence forced upon me by my spiritual shepherds from the inception of my writings.

This second issue concerns anti-Christ acts and traditions that we human beings have stupidly fabricated out of, I suspect, both the prevailing Greek philosophy that exalts reason over emotion and the Fathers' disregard of Jesus' words that instituted the Eucharist in the Blood of the new Covenant. Some fell back on the cleansed or saved and perhaps some of the gospel writers' subjective opinions, while others fell back on older covenants and traditions of the Jewish people, calling for bilateral performances by the people to repent by works and acts of faith. As a result of this initial or contributing cause, Pope Paul VI promulgated the Dogmatic Constitution on the Church (*Lumen Gentium*'s Ch. II, No. 9) to change the terms of God's personally formed covenant. It also changed the agreement from being one unilaterally performed by God, through the blood of Jesus Christ, to a bilateral contract to be performed by the good works of believers in Christ. The Covenant made-up is a *quid-pro-quo* deal, with the performance of a small flock of messianic people whose mission is to work with Christ to redeem the masses lost to perdition—obviously a less safe salvation than the original one unilaterally performed by God in Christ.

Let me start from the beginning and argue my case in hopes of adding light, instead of heat, to this controversy I try to raise. For openers, a simple reading of The Gospel According to John's reporting of the Last Supper in comparison to what Our Lord personally told Paul (1 Cor 11:25) and what Mathew, Mark, and Luke reported (Mt 26:26, Mk 14:24, and Lk 22:26) reveals the obvious contradiction. John not only ignores the words instituting the Eucharist, but nullifies the New Covenant as evidence of God's saving action in human history by not mentioning it and elsewhere insisting that God alone does not forgive us. According to John, we must forgive ourselves by faith and other works. Pope Benedict XVI previously contended that Jesus' words are "interdependent" with his death, and without them it is a meaningless execution. Death and words establish that the Blood of the Covenant forgives our iniquities. As Cardinal Joseph Ratzinger, however, he edited *God Is Near Us*, which at page 29 preaches the "interdependent" truth. In the same book, at pages 59 and 60, he preaches his inconsistent opinion that belies God's unilateral forgiveness of our evildoings. In response to his question of what form of a meal did Jesus mean to be the memorial supper, Ratzinger preached as follows:

Nowadays New Testament scholars essentially give one of two answers. Some of them say that the Eucharist of the early Church built upon meals that Jesus shared with his disciples day after day. Others say that the Eucharist is the *continuation of the meals with sinners* that Jesus had held. This second idea has become for many people a fascinating notion with far-reaching consequences. For it would mean that the Eucharist is the sinners' banquet, where Jesus sits at the table; the Eucharist is the public gesture by which he invites everyone without exception. The logic of this is expressed in a far-reaching criticism of the Church's Eucharist, since it implies that the Eucharist cannot be conditional on anything, not dependent on denomination or even on baptism. It is necessarily an open table to which all may come to encounter the universal God, without any limit or denominational preconditions. But then, again—however tempting the idea may be—it contradicts what we find in the Bible. Jesus' Last Supper was not one of those meals he held with "publicans and sinners." He made it subject to the basic form of the Passover, which implies that this meal was held in a family setting. Thus he kept it with his new family, with the Twelve; with those whose feet he washed, whom he had prepared, by his Word and by this cleansing of absolution (Jn 13:10), to receive a blood relationship with him, to become one body with him. The Eucharist is not itself the sacrament of reconciliation, but in fact it presupposes that sacrament. It is the *sacrament of the reconciled*, to which the Lord invites all those who have become part of his family. That is why, from the beginning, the Eucharist has been preceded by a discernment. We have just heard this, in very dramatic form, from Paul: Whoever eats unworthily, eats and drinks judgment on himself, because he does not distinguish the Body of the Lord (1 Cor 11:27 *ff*). The *Teaching of the Twelve Apostles*, one of the oldest writings outside the New Testament, from the beginning of the second century, takes up the apostolic tradition and has the priest, just before distributing the Sacrament, saying: "Whoever is holy, let him approach—whoever is not, let him do penance!" [miscites *Didache* 10:6] The Eucharist is—let us repeat it—the sacrament of those who have let themselves be reconciled by God, who have thus become members of his family and put themselves into his hands. That is why there are conditions for participating in it; it presupposes that we have voluntarily entered into the mystery of Jesus Christ.

Obviously, Ratzinger contradicts himself by disregarding the New Covenant performance of God purifying us, while he attempts to contradict the experts on the New Testament with his less competent opinion. Note that he leads off with John's version of a Last Supper event as an authoritative take on the Eucharist Covenant that John fails to mention. He cites St. Paul's letter to Corinth, but not for the definition that Our Lord personally gave to Paul about the Last Supper words that expressly mention the Eucharist and its New Covenant. Lastly, he reaches for straws and miscites *Didache* 10:6. Baptism is the 10:6 topic, while 9:5 deals with the Eucharist in *Didache*. It is not scripture, but just another traditional human precept. Its bigotry manifests in *Didache* 9:5.

But let no one eat or drink of this Eucharistic thanksgiving, but they that have been baptized into the name of the Lord, for concerning this also the Lord hath said: Give not that which is holy to the dogs.

Father Ratzinger later validated his opinion. As Cardinal Joseph Ratzinger, he oversaw that the *Catechism of the Catholic Church*, released in the mid-1990s, ruled that the Eucharist was a sacrament "not ordered" to forgive sin. He spoke for the Church not for Christ. Christ meant for it to forgive all sins. But, Ratzinger effectively silenced the New Testament scholars and theologians who disagreed with him until he became the Church's voice. One such silenced figure, a theology professor from Loyola University, L.A., lectured a lay ministry school that I attended in the early 1990s. She contended that those possessed of mortal sins should receive Holy Communion without any need of confession or Reconciliation because the Eucharist healed as we assume when we pray, ". . . but only say the word, and I shall be healed." Should she dare repeat her lecture today, she may be seeking work at Southern Methodist University.

Rather than risk another Vatican Council to clear up the misunderstanding, the Vatican chooses to use Bishop Synods where the curia and cardinals can control decisions. Thus, the Synod on the Eucharist had Vatican working documents directing the gathered bishops to allow Eucharist only to those of the faith. Consequently, my diocesan bishop returned from a Synod and promulgated statutes that exclude all but Catholics who are "in the state of grace, not be conscious of any grave sin and be fasting . . . ." He was extremely "obedient in faith" to the teaching of the Church and well-indoctrinated in the tradition back to Paul that only "worthy" Catholics are entitled to receive Eucharist. Later, *Sacramentum Caritatis* authorized him final judgment on this matter after Pope Benedict XVI delegated the most valuable of divine Church gifts to diocesan bishops.

Unlike my spiritual shepherds, when Jesus was confronted with the issue of his guests not washing their hands as Jews were traditionally supposed to do before eating meals, Jesus attacked the complaining hierarchy of his day (Mk 7:6-13), as follows:

> He said to them: "How accurately Isaiah prophesied about you hypocrites when he wrote,

> 'This people pays me lip service
> but their heart is far from me.
> Empty is the reverence they do me
> because they teach as dogmas
> mere human precepts.'

> You disregard God's commandment and cling to what is human tradition."

> He went on to say: "You have made a fine art of setting aside God's commandment in the interests of keeping your traditions! . . . That is the way you nullify God's word in favor of the traditions you have handed on."

Understand that there exists a reasonable and charitable discerning of Paul's warning that whoever "unworthily" consumes the body and blood of the Lord sins against the body and blood of the Lord. This warning mixes with "He who eats and drinks without recognizing the body, eats and drinks a judgment on himself." This excommunicates no one. But, both warnings advise examining our consciences to avoid Christ's post-salvation judgment on our discrimination, "but since it is the Lord who judges us, he chastens us to keep us from being condemned with the rest of the world." Simply, we are instructed to wait on and be considerate of each other, or Christ may chastise us later. Without presupposing more, this unbiased reading clearly shows the passage does not support excommunication, but it is Paul again teaching good manners.

Father George Smiga gave his lecture, *Biblical Roots of Eucharist*, in June, 2004 at John Carroll University. Bishop Anthony Pilla, the President of the U.S. Conference of Catholic Bishops later endorsed the lecture as being consistent with the "teachings of our faith." Fr. Smiga contended that Paul's warnings simply mean the sin was in breaking up the Christian fellowship, with the "body" as the symbol of unity among the Christians that is not recognized. We too are to be drawn into the insight that the blood of the Covenant has brought us together as One. Unworthiness happens to be our common trait, pardoned by God.

Both my pope and my retired diocesan bishop cited Paul's "unworthy" term as translated according to their own subjective opinions in order to exclude most of humanity from redemption as brothers and sisters of Christ. The exceptions are those who believe in Christ, are baptized in Christ, and are obedient to the Church's teachings. For example, Bishop Wiegand alone responded to my concerns, as follows:

The teaching of the Church is very clear since the time at least of St. Paul. To receive Holy Communion requires true Catholics faith and worthiness. You are simply incorrect in your analysis and need the "obedience of faith" to accept the teaching of the Church.

My answering letter stated that I instead had primary "obedience of faith" to the teaching of Christ, our sole teacher, and I asked for fatherly advice as to how my analysis was incorrect. In response I received an oppressive silence from him too, and I remain uncorrected.

Lumen Gentium, Ch. IV, No. 37 burdens me with the obligation to express my opinions concerning the good of the Church. It also expressly says that the spiritual shepherds will, attentively in Christ, consider with fatherly love the suggestions proposed by the laity. According to the document, a familiar dialogue was to result, and in this way the whole Church "may more effectively fulfill its mission for the life of the world." Instead, I get oppressive silence from my shepherds.

Since God certainly and perfectly performs the covenant pledges He made to teach and forgive us, the mission of the Church of Christ left by Jesus initially appears limited to consecrating and distributing the Eucharist for the life of the world. As God forgives all of our evildoing, the Blood of the Covenant, the Blood of the Lamb, redeems everyone created. Additionally, God teaches even the least of us all we need to know for everlasting salvation. Apparently, this does not include belief in Christ. However, proclaiming the passion and death of Jesus, regardless of belief in him as Christ, likely is an essential part of the memorial Eucharist.

A key to the Church's additional role in teaching the rest of humanity about Eucharist matters is the final pledge that God makes in the New Covenant:

and I will remember their sin no more.

The risen Christ presumably instructed Paul personally about the Lord's Supper as well as the final judgment we will all face before him after our redemption to everlasting life. Christ, all-knowing, will weigh our merits and demerits from faith to works, and He will mercifully judge if we are to be temporarily chastised to perfect us to live together in everlasting bliss. The necessary implication or conclusion to be drawn from this judgment is that God's perfect forgiveness of our iniquities leaves some mysterious residual for Jesus Christ to justly deal with. Since he is already our advocate in heaven and knows our good to weigh with our evil, we could not ask for a better judge or more trustworthy chastiser.

However, the Roman Catholic Church also negates the New Covenant relationship with God and denies that God alone performs the forgiving of our evildoing and the teaching of all we need to know for our salvation. The opening page of *Lumen Gentium*, Ch. II, No. 9, purportedly the Dogmatic Constitution on the Church, a document of Vatican II as promulgated by His Holiness, Pope Paul VI on November 21, 2964, proves this when simply read as follows:

CHAPTER II
On the People of God

9. At all times and in every race God has given welcome to whoever fears him and does what is right (cf. Acts 10:35). God, however, does not make men holy and save them merely as individuals, without bond or link between one another. Rather has it pleased him to bring men together as one people, a people which acknowledges him in truth and serves him in holiness. He therefore chose the race of Israel as a people unto himself. With it he set up a covenant. Step by step he taught and prepared this people, making known in its history both himself and the decree of his will and making it holy unto himself. All these things, however, were done by way of preparation and as a figure of the new and perfect covenant, which was to be ratified in Christ, and of that fuller revelation which was to be given through the word of God himself made flesh. "Behold the days shall come says the Lord, and I will make a new covenant with the House of Israel, and with the house of Judah . . . I will give my law in their bowels, and I will write it in their heart, and I will be their God, and they shall be my people . . . For all of them shall know me, from the least of them even to the greatest, says the Lord" (Jer 31:31-34). Christ instituted this New Covenant, the New Testament, that is to say, in his Blood (cf. 1 Cor 11:25), calling together a people made up of Jew and Gentile, making them one, not according to the flesh but in the Spirit.

This was to be the new People of God. <u>For those who believe in Christ</u>, who are reborn not from a perishable but from an imperishable seed. (Emphasis mine.)

Word-by-word, compare the quoted portion of page 18 No. 9 of *Lumen Gentium* to the correctly quoted New Covenant at pages 3 and 4 of this sequel. The man-made deletions are blatant. The scribe's first phrase immediately after the quote is an untruth, "Christ instituted *this* New Covenant, this New Testament, that is to say, in his Blood (cf. 1 Cor 11:25) . . ." (Italics mine). The Jesuits taught me that a lie was speech contrary to thought, and since the writers knew that "this" was their fabrication of God's New Covenant, they lied. Christ died for God's Covenant, not *this* one.

Those who dared to delete God's New Covenant markedly worsened their culpability by the blasphemy, the anti-Christ declarations, that attempts to negate evidence of God's saving in history. It nullifies the fact that Jesus Christ is our savior and redeemer. That covenant gave mankind a new relationship, a new kingdom, with God's unilateral performance. It assured salvation of every one of us by God's simple goodness. They substitute Catholics who believe in Christ for God and Christ when it comes to world redemption. Christians are now the new messianic people who will redeem the rest of humanity from the perdition to which the Church appears to condemn them.

The anti-Christ blasphemy appears in the deliberate acts of the Catholic Church. Such blasphemy may disregard the evidence of God and Christ fully performing the New Covenant and redeeming the world. To compound the error, it substitutes Christ's messianic task to human believers in Christ. These believers, presumably baptized Catholics in good stead, are now delegated the task to help Jesus redeem the rest of the wayward masses destined to perdition because they were not lucky enough to be selected or destined as Catholics. The Church obviously ignores the New Covenant and Christ's part in establishing it.

His Holiness Pope John XXIII was, as most of us know, a different sort of person, and had he lived, this document of Vatican II would not exist as such. However, he died in 1963, and Pope Paul VI promulgated *Lumen Gentium*'s chapter II in late 1964. By that time, the curia was released and allowed to participate, likely to be made up of the scribes who dared distort God's New Covenant and alter the Testament of Christ as defined by human precepts. We now inherit that Testament. Pope John deliberately restrained the curia. In fact, he made it an issue to be decided as to what role, if any, the curia was to have in the Church. This document justifies the restraints.

I respectfully suggest that the Gospel of John unintentionally was an anti-Christ document from its inception. Whoever wrote John's Gospel, the authorship is attributed to John the apostle. The author may be members of the cult that came from Ephesus. The Prologue shows Hellenist influence. The Greek's mythology of gods coupling with earthbound women to produce offspring appealed to John's writers, and a few fathers in the early Church used that to help explain Christology. Much is my speculation, but in preparing his Last Supper painting, Leonardo Da Vinci made a sketch of the young apostle John asleep on his arms, resting on the table. The sketch is lodged in a London museum. It better explains to me why John's Gospel reports nothing of Jesus' words at the Last Supper, words that gave meaning to the otherwise meaningless execution of Jesus. As a result, John's Gospel nullifies or negates both the New Covenant's fulfillment in the blood of Christ and God's lone performance of our New Covenant redemption in Christ simply out of His goodness.

John's Gospel's Bread of Life passages more likely deal with the nourishment of doing God's will that Jesus claimed sustained him at the Samaritan's well. But, since John's Gospel overlooks the fact that God Himself saves us without any need of faith or works on our part, it burdens us with its own religious explanation for our conducting of a bilateral covenant as Jews had from the past. The surrounding religion's traditions of sacrifice to please God called for belief in Christ. Thus, John's Gospel, probably in good conscience, reasoned to the need of belief in Christ and other submissions to be saved.

The Gospel, epistle, and Revelation of whoever writes under the moniker "John" have seduced the Catholic Church to reject the New Covenant teachings of Christ, Paul, and the Synoptics in favor of accepting "John" as truth. Origen (date circa 220) may have been correct in saying John factually was a liar, but he too praised the *Logos* spirituality theme. An earlier father of the Church Policarp claimed that the apostle John converted him, and this claim biased Policarp's student Iraneaus (date circa 200), later the Bishop of Lyons, France, into selecting "John's" gospel with those of Matthew, Mark, and Luke to be our four book Canon. He trashed all other gospels even that of Thomas whose theme focused interiorly, perhaps consistent with God's imprinted truths in us. He limited them to four gospels to conform to the four corners of the earth.

St. Ambrose figures large in later history of Eucharistic sacrifice. He was the architect of the Latin Mass which is still practiced today. He also mentored St. Augustine and was around after Constantine fabricated our monarchic Church. Augustine's biases for Plato and the idea that government is operated best by ruling elitists put another nail in democracy's coffin. Jesus proscribed to our leaders that they not rule us as gentiles do. Today, we not only are ruled in the Church as Gentiles did in Christ's day, but we are indoctrinated to accept faith and good works from the teachings of the Gospel According to John and the *Dogmatic Constitution* of *Lumen Gentium,* Ch. II as our standards of religious conduct.

St. Ambrose confessed to receiving Eucharist often because he sinned often. He sounds familiar to me in that respect. He intended to be baptized on his deathbed so those Holy Communions were not likely received by a baptized Ambrose. He obviously assumed the Eucharist forgave sins, as there was no easy reconciliation at the time. A Dominican priest told me that they persuaded Ambrose to be baptized when they appointed him bishop of Milan. Since Ambrose was intimately involved with the Latin Mass, he must have studied the Eucharistic Prayer mentioning the cup of blood, the blood of the New Covenant, shed to forgive our sins. One would think he would call to the Church's attention that the New Covenant does away with need for John the Baptist's water cure. And maybe he did. But, perhaps it was too early in our evolution for us to grasp that the Church, with exception of the Eucharist, was not needed to teach nor forgive. The fact that his student Augustine made up the Original Sin Doctrine from his arguments with Pelagius shows that it would have been difficult to sell the New Covenant concept. A millennium later, the inquisition was a sword hanging over every free thinker's head to quiet anything other than *status quo* thinking. The Church to this day has a department assigned that purpose.

Note the quote of No. 9 *Lumen Gentium* at the bottom of page 18, where the scribes nosedive into claiming that "those who believe in Christ" are those reborn and redeemed chosen by God. This claim contradicts God's Covenant and God's pledge to forgive people's evildoings. But the contradiction's negation of the evidence of Christ's redemption of the world permits the Catholic Church to claim that we Catholics are the righteous and others are wrong and condemned. They may be crusaded against, tortured, and denied Holy Communion as unworthy human beings. The Church pays Christ lip service while it disregards God's law of loving each other impartially in favor of clinging to these human opinions and traditions that negate God's New Covenant.

Pope John XXIII stepped in between Pope Pius XII and Pope Paul VI to return Catholicism to its true Church foundation. The latter had his cardinal cap inadvertently delayed when Pope Pius XII died, and Pope John was to be an interim and insignificant substitute while his successor Montini was prepared. There is an element behind the scene of Catholic traditionalists who feel they know best for the Church, and they maneuvered those to their likings to be "elected" to the Vatican. Pope John XXIII, however, was a God-given blessing, and in the short lifetime he had left, he aimed the Catholic Church toward being a global church, true to its title and the way Christ intended. He gathered the bishops from around the world and called the Second Vatican Council. He restrained the curia, made their role an issue to be decided, and he did away with the oaths against modern thinking and having to obey the Church magisterium. Thus, the pope, the bishops, and their theologians were free to think and discuss the matters close to their hearts and minds concerning the good of the Church in its mission for the life of the world.

I hope the faith convictions that I heatedly espouse are those imprinted in my heart and mind by our Lord. I hope they are from the competency of my experiences. And I hope the daily consumption of the Real Presence in Holy Communion might have inspired them. I realize that everyone is touched differently and that I tend toward self-righteousness in representing the causes of so many people harmed or denied their God-given rights by the Catholic corporate institution, which also offends me with its oppressive silence.

I have come to believe that my Catholic Church is not true to the Church of Christ in its exclusive Eucharist, which denies the God-given right to receive Holy Communion by God's forgiveness of evildoing in the New Covenant. Today, I mostly attribute the problem to Pope Benedict XVI. But, the negation of God's New Covenant is a Church-wide harm, and it needs the whole Church of Christ to cure it. My unanswered letters have certainly proved my inadequacy in fraternal correction!

In concern for my Roman Catholic Church, this disregard of the New Covenant relationship with God and its negation of Christ's teachings to support the theme mostly presented by the Gospel According to John frightens me far more. But because the condition has existed for centuries, one wonders whether the Lord is concerned. Critical thinking has led me to question even Matthew's Gospel's quote of Jesus, "I will entrust to you the keys of the kingdom of heaven. Whatever you declare bound on earth shall be bound in heaven; whatever you declare loosed on earth shall be loosed in heaven." Can Peter reject the New Covenant of Paul, Matthew, Mark, and Luke to bind us to these other ideas and those of the Gospel According to John? Most, if not all, Christian religions have succumbed to John's Gospel as being inspired by God and not merely being human opinions. For near two millenniums, the Holy Spirit, who supposedly oversees us, has allowed the Catholic Church to apparently overrule God and Christ's New Covenant dealings as well as its proof in God's saving action in favor of the teachings in John's Gospel. A questionably stable Pope IX dictated that Peter can speak infallibly. Is John's Gospel thus confirmed? We may hear such fictions from Popes Paul, John Paul, and Benedict in their insistence that the exclusive Eucharist and the writings of "John" remain the teachings of the Roman Church. But, since my spiritual leaders will not answer my letters, I am left to my own convictions.

I placed my confidence in Pope Benedict XVI's repentance to exercise ressourcement and return the Catholic Church to identification with the Church of Christ that Jesus had in mind. I knew from page 93 of Father Haring's *My Hope for the Church* that Father Joseph Ratzinger was one of two protagonists, the other being Karol Wojtyla, who used media propaganda to accept Vatican II principles only in modified versions while selling their own restrictive interpretations. If the Spirit of Christ moves him to act, I believe Pope Benedict can switch sides in the controversy, and he has abilities to remedy his wrongdoing, even if it is in opposition to Church politics.

Thus, when confronted by the New Testament scholars' criticism of the exclusive Eucharist and their learned contentions that Christ's scriptural teachings intended an open Eucharist, regardless of denomination and having no conditions of worthiness, we see Father Joseph Ratzinger preaching to the contrary. On his likely less credible expertise, he makes Bible translations beginning with the Gospel of John's washing of feet. His poorer argument succeeds over the New Testament scholars. It shows his willingness to use might over right to get his way in controversies.

Earlier than his teaming up with Karol Wojtyla, he enthusiastically championed the openness of Vatican II, and he even wrote a book on his views. From 1964 to 1969, something occurred to change his views. A hearsay or rumor has it that his students trashed his apartment in those years of juvenile unrest. Professor of Theology, Ronald Modras, was a student of Ratzinger the winter of 1968/1969, and he wrote an article, aided by a 152-page typescript of Professor Ratzinger's lecture notes. According to Modras and confirmed by the notes, Ratzinger agreed with Hans Küng that Jesus did not intend to found a church. Ratzinger situated the Church of Christ's foundation in the Last Supper words, where Jesus linked the paschal lamb, the suffering servant, and the new covenant themes with the "for many" of Mark's Gospel 14:24. Ratzinger expressly taught that the "for many" expression of Jesus prevents the church from becoming simply a select community of the righteous, a community that condemns the wayward masses to perdition.

However, that is specifically what the self-righteous of the Catholic Church do in *Lumen Gentium* Ch. II, No. 9. They claim to simply be a select community of the righteous, those who believe in Christ. That community condemns the rest of humanity to perdition, unless Catholics trouble themselves to redeem the non-believers. Of course, to reach this status Catholics had to do away with believing in the terms and provisions of God as made in His New Covenant. They also did away with the belief that Jesus redeems of the world, replacing Him with this self-selected messianic people. It raises Catholics by their own bootstraps to compete as messianic redeemers of the world with Jesus Christ, the Son that God selected as Savior.

Earlier in life Joseph Ratzinger wrote his doctoral dissertation on St. Augustine's ideas about the People of God. From his mentor Augustine, Ratzinger learned to translate the Bible according to a charity yardstick and to discern scripture ambiguities against what was more charitable. Ratzinger exemplifies the rule in his doctoral thesis on Donatists. As Bishop of Hippo, Augustine confronted the Donatist culture in North Africa. Donatist priests surrendered their scriptures to Roman persecutors, and the Donatists thereafter refused their sacraments on the basis that they were infected. Augustine argued their rejection of the priests showed a lack of the fundamental Christian virtue of charity, and the lack of charity defined Donatism as not of Christ's Church. Then, young Ratzinger's thought dictated that the true Church could not be founded on the exclusion of others. The doctoral thesis is another inconsistent thinking with his excommunication of "many," which leads me to believe that Pope Benedict tends to change convictions.

My pastor, Joseph Bishop, once told me that clergymen avoided putting their thoughts in writing because an idea might return to haunt them in their hierarchical climbing. In the case of Pope Benedict XVI, we have much writing to compare for inconsistencies, allowing for the hope for the Church expressed by Father Haring. It is my hope, too.

Based on these hopes, and the hope from his talents that once were described by a journalist whose interview revealed "Ratzinger at work, wielding proof texts that in his hand are as powerful, and as malleable, as articles of the Constitution in the hands of an ideologically partisan jurist," we could not ask for a better fixer of the Church. The popes who succeeded Pope John XXIII have placed the Catholic Church in the traditional state that it was in prior to Vatican II, and as a result, the Church of Christ does not subsist in the Catholic Church.

Consider inviting Muslims to share Holy Communion. They may hear of Jesus' excruciating suffering to ransom them for everlasting life, and thereby be stirred. I understand they respect Jesus as a prophet like Mohammed. But, they believe Jesus never died, nor do they believe that he is God. Yet, their awareness of what Jesus sacrificed for them, in shedding the Blood of the Covenant, may, on receipt of Holy Communion, transform them to be one with us. They may retain their beliefs and simply share the Eucharist. We should let them and God meet at our Lord's Supper, and Christ can carry on from there as he may have intended when he left us his Real Presence.

In respect to his inept argument telling Islam to be more reasonable, Pope Benedict XVI should have learned that he and the Catholic Church cannot teach those of other faith convictions. People generally cannot be taught contrary to their own judgments, but they can learn on their own. God knows best, and so He pledged to imprint in us how to know Him and how to know His law of love. So, we should open the Eucharist to allow God's grace to work. God imprinted Himself in our hearts and minds, using the Eucharistic sacrifice as a means. From the beginning, God gave us the Eucharist so we can hear the story of the excruciating passion of Jesus, and He also gave it to establish His new covenant relationship with all of us. To appreciate Jesus, we were to hear the actual story, not the Gospel According to John's version. God, emptied of His divinity to be fully man, shows us how to know God, love God, and serve God. Aware of such a stirringly told story, we and our Jewish and Muslim siblings could further appreciate Jesus Christ as we consume Him. From within, He intimately transforms us to know, love, and serve Our Lord and all the rest of humanity, whom Jesus' death has redeemed to everlasting life.

Pope Benedict XVI, like Peter with Cornelius, cannot deem what God has made pure and worthy in the Blood of the Covenant to be unworthy to receive Christ in Eucharist. Everyone's evildoings are forgiven, entitling them to "take this!" All I see today preventing this from occurring is the obstinacy in the heart and mind of Pope Benedict XVI and the Church he controls. When Benedict disregarded my many expressions of concern to him, Passionist Father Newbold, C.P. spiritually directed me to wait for another pope. But, I knew I was too limited in time and ability to seek another. Besides, with the help of the Holy Spirit, I think this one is God's choice. I fear that he may not be awakened to his call. If senility sets in or one of the other disabling conditions prevents him, he may not accomplish what I believe he knows he should do. I pray to God to help Pope Benedict XVI to, with moral courage, overcome his ego, pride in judgments, and any sense of allegiance he feels he owes his associates for choosing and supporting him to the papacy. I pray that he overcomes these things to do what he ought to do as Vicar of Christ, what he ought to do simply as Joseph Ratzinger, our brother in Christ.

The Catholic Church uncharitably condemned "the many" to perdition from the Fourth Lateran Council in 1215, confirming that "the ones will receive perpetual punishment with the devil" were not merely a few. Later in 1442, the Council of Florence made the custom of Baptism law and asserted that many are damnable, "The holy Roman Church . . . firmly believes, professes and proclaims that none of those outside of the Catholic Church, not Jews, not heretics, can participate in eternal life, but will go into the eternal fire prepared for the devil and his angels, unless they are brought into it (the Catholic Church) before the end of life" (DS 1820). To Catholics, Pope Benedict XII also declared in the Constitution *Benedictus Deus* (1536), "We define that according to the general disposition of God the souls of those who die in actual mortal sin go down immediately after death into hell and are there tormented by the pains of hell." The lot of "the many" is not improved with the Pope Paul VI signed *Lumen Gentium* (1964) continuing our traditions and disregarding God's commandment of love. On the other hand, the Second Vatican Council of Pope John XXIII sensibly admitted that even atheists attain eternal salvation. It did so without expressly revoking or correcting the previous statements, such as those of the Council of Florence, which presumably is infallible. But Pope John died, and many questions not discussed or resolved at Vatican II are asked of Pope Benedict XVI and us siblings of Christ. Where are we now?

My grandson, Bertrand Ithurburn, is helping me write this summer. He is being schooled in Long Beach in creative writing, and because of my vision disability I am leaning on him. Bertrand is a name in my maternal family tree where appears a newsworthy Bertrand d'Echauz of Baigorri. He was a bishop who took over the judgment against Basque priests for witchcraft after forty of them were burnt at the stake by the Inquisition. No priests were executed after he sat in judgment. On my father's side, the family name has a more recent history of notables, such as Caetano Ithurburu, who was the poet laureate of the international Lincoln Brigade, defeated by Franco and the fascists. His daughter, "Negrita" was the "puppy-love" of "Che" Guevara. Recently, I heard that nineteen Ithurburu cousins disappeared in Argentina's dirty war. So, on both sides of my family we have free thinkers and active liberators of society. My grandson has names to wear with respect. Ithurburn is an Ellis Island aberration because a bureaucrat made our last "u" become an "n." In Basque, the meaning of "Ithur" is flowing water. I hope that from this spring streams of Christ's waters will flow to renew the world.

3. *CHURCH OF CHRIST'S WAY*

Jesus Christ never got His way with His Eucharist as it was always limited by humans in its distribution. Traditionally, the Roman Catholic Church required "worthiness" based on an uncharitable translation of a letter from St. Paul, and later it reasoned that recipients must be baptized. For a time, the Second Vatican Council returned the Church to what Christ intended—open and universal with no reasonable conditions attached—but our present Pope, Benedict XVI, was the prime mover in keeping it exclusive to those baptized and voluntarily reconciled according to his scriptural reasoning.

The story of Jesus has not entirely been told. He tried so hard to tell us that God Almighty loves us just as we are, so we would be at peace and free to develop ourselves by self-realization and experience in this world. But, we insist on reasoning to explain God's way of salvation, such as defining "transubstantiation" to explain the bread that Jesus says is his body. We distrust accepting Christ at His word alone, and the story of Jesus thusly appears to have failed in history. He was crucified in Jerusalem two millennia ago. His final utterances on the cross were cries of abandonment or meaningless. He apparently died alone, separate from God. However, His followers remain around with a continuing story.

From His mother, who kept record by heart, we are aware that Jesus was called from infancy to trust in God's love. He grew in wisdom and, as we all do, learned from experience that God loved everyone impartially. Thus, where He once expressed His bigotry that non-Jews were "dogs," He learned better and volunteered to die in martyrdom for every human created. From the days of learning at His mother's knee, Jesus was aware, and in praying reflections on the scriptures He learned that He was linked to the paschal lamb (Ex 12). He was to be the suffering servant giving Himself up "for many" (Is 53), and He was to be the mediator of the New Covenant (Jer 31). He learned that His mission was to be crucified and thusly demonstrate God's message of love to the world, triumphing over evil in human hearts by performing the New Covenant in His shedding of blood.

The story that His followers had to relate afterward began at supper several hours before His crucifixion. He had repeated to His followers His prediction that He would rise from death in three days. As predicted, those who tended to believe Him witnessed Him on our first Easter. He appeared different, but He revealed Himself to be Jesus, alive and with wounds intact. Thereafter, reflecting on Jesus' crucifixion and His words at His Last Supper, we gain meaning to His mission and realize that the words and death are mutually interdependent in our understanding of what happened and what is happening, as time and space are arrested, to make our Eucharistic sacrifices one piece with the events of that weekend in Jerusalem.

Being a student of scripture, Jesus saw evil in the world that began in human hearts. He learned that God promised a New Covenant with His people, whereby, in time, God would unilaterally perform pledges of teaching everyone how to know God and His commandment of loving each other. Additionally, God promised to forgive everyone's evildoing and forget their sin forever. To demonstrate God's performance in Christ and activate His saving action in history, Jesus instituted His Eucharist in thanks of the Covenant.

In the words of the Last Supper, words that the world-redeeming death of Jesus gave meaning, we have included what institutes the Eucharist. As recorded by Paul, Mark, Matthew, and Luke, the New and Everlasting Covenant had this essential part. Professor Ratzinger lectured that the words "for many" (Mk 14:24) prevent the church from becoming simply a select community of the righteous—a community that condemns the wayward masses to perdition. But as Pope Benedict XVI today, he steers our church another way. He artfully disregards the New Covenant and deliberately delegates to conditioned diocesan bishops the onerous task of denying most humans the Church's Eucharist.

Both the story Jesus tried to tell of a New Covenant that God Himself performed simply out of goodness and the Eucharistic means of imprinting the knowledge of God and His law of love—with the accompanying forgiveness received in the Real Presence—are being uncharitably nullified in order to cling to human tradition and reasoning. By mere human precepts, the Catholic Church negates the evidence of God's saving action in history. But God, through Christ, fulfills His pledges, and He performs the New Covenant in the world in spite of our efforts that apparently negate His re-creations in the eyes of humans.

Pope Benedict's refusal to share the Lord's Supper with non-Catholics and non-reconciled Catholics reminds me of Peter scrupulously refusing to eat with the Gentile Cornelius. Three times Our Lord had to tell Peter that what God made clean no man must say is unclean to share a meal. Earlier, Jesus criticized His hierarchy for hypocritically insisting that His guests clean in traditional ways before sharing his meal. He said that it disregarded God's law of loving each other in favor of clinging to man-made traditions of cleansing. In Pope Benedict's case, he stands in the shoes of both Peter and the hierarchy of Jesus when he insists on baptism and reconciliations to better clean what the Blood of the Covenant made pure.

As we were going to press this summer, Pope Benedict XVI released *Caritatis in Veritate* (Charity in Truth), his third encyclical letter and his first social one. Our pessimistic Augustinian leader offers an Aquinas optimism, reasoning for ethically governing our social economy and global capitalist markets. Crediting his predecessor Blessed John XXIII with the idea of need for a true world political authority, Benedict suggests regulating the world so that the family of nations can acquire teeth for the common good and secure human development inspired by values of charity in truth. It is surmised that the letter is built on centuries of papal social teachings, but the skepticism it has about the Church affecting the benevolence of unregulated markets, whose god is more likely a monetary one, suffers a lack of trust in human reasoning, even reasons obviously as trustworthy as those from our Pope, who claims support from Blessed John XXIII. I wrote Pope Benedict, telling him that human powers and reasoning are not enough. As for teeth, I would think his experiences with Hitler would negate that. I wrote letters in order to communicate with Pope Benedict XVI and my spiritual shepherds about concerns I had for the good of the Church, hoping that it "may more effectively fulfill its mission for the life of the world" (*Lumen Gentium*, No. 37) by means of an open Eucharist. It is plainly seen that Pope Benedict's social teachings to our world capitalists and entrepreneurs may be part of the Church's mission, but it is a peripheral obligation if one at all. However, Pope Benedict has chosen to go it alone and disregard God's New Covenant, wherein God unilaterally imprints how to know His law of love in the hearts and minds of all human beings. Benedict denies the universal Eucharist, whereby God brings His Real Presence home to all of us here on earth. The inclusive Eucharist was instituted for everyone to hear Our LORD's story of love. If Our Holy Father tends to his job as Pope and lets God's people go to Holy Communion as Jesus directed, then Pope Benedict would do far better with regulating the market and strengthening a world political authority with love rather than teeth. He would stand in the shoes of Christ and leave humanity to run its own market with only God's imprinted law of love to govern them. To make the teeth in laws effective can be left to men.

Among my letters in mid-March, I told my spiritual shepherds of former British Prim Minister Tony Blair teaching at Yale in order to enhance global harmony. He argued that "there are limits to humanism and beyond those limits God and only God can work." Obviously, Pope Benedict ignores this writing too and feels his own academic suggestions toward what he calls "Christian humanism" will be more effective for fulfilling the Church's mission for the life of the world. Based on human precepts that have not proven very effective for millenniums, he chooses to nullify God in His New Covenant and God in His inclusive Eucharist to work beyond the limits of humanism.

At the UN General assembly last year, Pope Benedict addressed their duty to uphold human rights. Again drawing on the credibility of John XXIII, he told the assembly that failure to protect against violations of peoples' rights—one of which we in the USA hold to be true is freedom of religion—makes governing bodies illegitimate. It necessarily follows that people of all faith denominations, and even those without faith convictions, are entitled to the gift of Christ's Eucharist while retaining their own convictions. Since they are the people of God to whom Christ extended God's New Covenant, the blood of the Covenant has purified them, and God forgives their iniquities—their evildoings. Each is worthy of the Lord's Supper, just as Cornelius was worthy of Peter's meal. Denying anyone the Church's Eucharist denies Catholicism true Church status, and, according to Pope Benedict, bastardizes its government.

Christianity's impact, in spite of Catholics disregarding the New Covenant and its open Eucharist, has been spiritually global because of the New Covenant effectiveness from the time of Jesus Christ's crucifixion in Israel. Syrian Christians were in China's courts when Marco Polo visited, but Christians, especially Messianic Catholics, have made little impact on China and India since then. However, according to two decades of Chinese scholars' studies of Christian history, they recently concluded:

> The Christian moral foundation of social and cultural life was what made possible the emergence of capitalism and then the successful transition to democratic politics. We don't have any doubt about this.

The national attitude of the youth of China indicates that it has been influenced by this Christian awareness, but they still tend not to accept any foreign influence that tries to rule over their traditions in an outside way. They will do it their own way. Confucius posed a problem because he felt that China's values and cultures should not be influenced by its trade and commerce. So in about 1492, China burnt its fleet and went into 500 years of withdrawal, focusing inwardly. Their evolution to the present times may make them ripe to hear of Christ's Eucharist and New Covenant. Many were also influenced by Communism and Mao. They may now be susceptible to accepting Christ or His New Covenant to replace Maoism as an acceptable life morality. They appear to be potential Church of Christ members, susceptible to Christ's actual presence if we freely share His Eucharist. Mao's absence as a respected elder or teacher may be filled by Christ. The Chinese situation raises a question, one discussed at Vatican II, about ending the traditional Catholic Church's persistence in its feudalistic monarchy and lordly ruling over others as the Gentiles did in Jesus' time. We in the USA are scandalized by both the recent history of the Church hierarchy covering up child abuses for the purpose of saving face and, more recently, in condoning a Holocaust denying bishop for the sake of preserving the Church's numbers of Catholic sheep. The USA violently revolted against a monarch ruler and his divine rights of kings so we could conscientiously rule ourselves and insure ourselves God-given rights when those rights were being withheld from us. The world has inhaled this spirit of democracy from our experience, and China shows interest. Those hints from Pope Pius XII and the Catholic Church in Pope John's Vatican II may indicate that both China and Church are open to each other. Catholics democratically followed common sense and their informed consciences to resist the lordly rule of *Humanae Vitae*, evidencing that they know how to freely act. The possibility of a spiritually democratic China avoiding its Communist government feeds my more remote hope that a future Church of Christ might moreso subsist in the Chinese Catholic Church, to have it manage Christ's vineyard because our traditionalists in Rome are mismanaging it and fear updating to the modern advances of Pope John XXIII and his Council. If the Spirit has the true Church appear elsewhere, then the Church's Eucharist in China could be an authentic one, and we can do without Rome's rule, which denies Eucharist from many and deceives us about the New and Everlasting Covenant.

Today, there exists an asphalt road from about Cairo extending south as far as South Africa. It was built by Africans and Chinese together. Perhaps China's studies of the Christian moral principles and the aftereffects of God's relationship in the New Covenant played a part in this joint effort. China invested its technology and capital in exchange for African's labor and resources to build a road down the African Continent that both peoples can take pride in doing together. The new openness to the world was the hope of Vatican II, but our contribution as a Church—uncharitably excluding others—has not been to publicly share Christ in Eucharist nor Covenant. We did serve another gnat of advice—that contraceptives increase the AIDS problem in Africa. I submit that silence would have won more hearts than such advice.

I am not able to imagine all of the changes in history that would have likely occurred had the early Church fathers understood and applied the New Covenant and God's redemption of the world in Jesus Christ, assuring a continued inclusive Gift of Eucharist. However, common knowledge affords me speculations that the Jewish people would more likely accept the more inclusive religion as a continuation of their own. Then, Mohammed may have felt welcomed and not needing to look elsewhere than the Church of Christ in its Judeo-Christian joinder of a religion, as he was equally loved. The Greek and Roman Catholics would find no dispute in what law God imprinted because they would agree on the basic one, and no crusade would have sacked Constantinople. The Protestants would have no incentive to protest or dispute the one Church of Christ on legal grounds of faith or scriptura solo, because we would not insist on lording over them. Today, the self same New Covenant and open Eucharist remains extended by God as gifts to mankind without limits to humanity, but a lot of fanatical bias has harmed our ability to love each other. Free to disdain the offer to do it Christ's way, Christians still might choose to do it their own religious ways and thusly prevent the peace Christ intended to bring to the world forever. However, I respectfully suggest that if we share and consume God's heavenly bread with each other daily, Our Lord Jesus Christ will be employed to transform everyone to his Church's way, just as He seems to have planned to do from the beginning before we messed it up.

God's way is not our way. Christians refuse to accept this truism. Blessed John XXIII and assembled bishops acknowledged it as typical Catholics refused to acknowledge the Church's error even in matters of faith and morals. As a result, according to Catholic theologians, Christianity's reputation as being "the most murderous religion that has been" remains. To be a global Church of Christ and to successfully invite everyone to the Church's Eucharist, we have to overcome this past to be trusted. Today, from matters of religion to the cover ups for Bishops who protect sex abusers, we see the reluctance of our spiritual shepherds in acknowledging their fallibility, and they subsequently repeat their faults. The ressourcement of Vatican II meant to return us to Christ's way of living and loving each other. No one can say that Jesus Christ willed any of this wrongdoing. But, it was mostly done in His name, when it should be credited to our institutional churches. Today, as a claimed representative of Jesus Christ in His universal Church of Christ, His Holiness Pope Benedict XVI is called to vicariously do what Christ and Blessed John XXIII tried to do, admit our wrongdoing to others, and truly be God's Christ on earth. A suitable olive branch would remind us all that Christ's invitation to His Supper long awaits everyone.

Jesus Christ fulfilled the New Covenant in shedding His blood, and the kingdom of God was presented to us. The Lord's Prayer acknowledges "thy kingdom come, thy will be done on earth as it is in heaven." The new relationship of God and humanity began that Easter weekend, and God became one with us in Christ on earth. Humanity's future is Heaven, which is God forever in Himself! God imprinted in each individual's conscience how to know these truths as He wills. He has graced us to love each other in Christ. Tragically, this fundamental virtue of charity has been lacking in the Roman Catholic Church ever since they excluded human beings from their version of the New Covenant that Jesus purchased in His blood. The true Church could not subsist in the Church's exclusion of others. However, in spite of the Catholic Church's millennia of anti-Christ activity, the Church of Christ exists, and the invitation for every human being to take and eat then take and drink as Jesus directed continues to exist. His message is being told, and the limit or receipt of His gift is solely each person's reluctance to receive, solely distrusting in Jesus' words to do so.

Once the many share in Holy Communion, and the Real Presence transforms them as the Lord devised, we may enjoy the Church of Christ as it moreso subsists in the Roman Catholic Church. I respectfully submit that the world will be better for it, and the Catholic Church will be closer to being true Church. In my first letters and first book, *God's Gift To You*, I tried to persuade His Holiness Pope Benedict XVI to open his heart and mind to share God's Real Presence in Christ's Eucharist with every human being created. I met with no success of which I am aware, and the Church's Eucharist remains exclusive. The Church of Christ fails to subsist to that extent in the Catholic Church. Thereafter, from April 2008 to date I have sought to persuade Pope Benedict and his hierarchy to a more reasonable argument. In proving that God's New Covenant has cleansed humans of iniquity in Christ's blood, I have proven beyond a reasonable doubt and to a moral certainty that we all are worthy to receive Eucharist with no strings attached.

Plainly, it is not too late for us to remedy the wrongdoing of the Roman Catholic Church. It surprises me that no one already yelled "foul!" in the time elapsed. But, the trust Catholics have in the Church allowed for the fraud to be concealed and continued. In Vatican II, Pope John XXIII showed us how to return the Church to the global one Christ intended. He called a Council of assembled bishops, curbed the inner traditional government of the Church, and allowed free dialogue between pope, bishops, theologians, and competent people of God. Most importantly, he restrained the curia—the inner government of the Church—and removed oaths against modernizing and such, so there could be free and heartfelt dialogue between pope and bishops to return the Church to what Christ had in mind when He died and fulfilled the Covenant intended from our beginnings. Christ meant to establish the New Covenant and leave us the gift of the Eucharist to nourish all made clean by God's covenantal pledge. The early Church's Bishop of Lyon's sentimental selection of the writings of "John" and the Bishops of Rome's recent fabrication and maintenance of Church tradition in their own misrepresentation of God's New Covenant allows Catholics to arguably exclude "many" from both the Church of Christ's membership and Christ's Eucharist. Inadvertently, they negate the evidence of God's saving action. We may correct these wrongdoings. If Pope Benedict XVI or any of his successors lack the moral courage to do the will of God in the face of traditionalist pressures, then it calls for members of the Church of Christ to act for fraternal correction. The People of God can overrule a pope, especially when an anti-Christ wrongdoing, such as negating evidence of God's salvation of humanity, needs remedy. The body of the People of God has the same God-given right to overrule any member of the Church of Christ. "The entire body of the faithful . . . cannot err in matters of belief" when they show universal agreement (*Lumen Gentium*, Ch. II, No. 12). God imprinted common knowledge of how to know His law in each and all of us. Jesus demonstrated the cure for when basic rights are violated with both the fig tree and the commercial temple users. The violence we see exercised by Jesus need not be repeated. Instead, we should do as Pope John XXIII demonstrated at Vatican II—renew the Church in the Risen Christ's way. First on the agenda of this nonviolent and democratic change should be amending our Constitution to truthfully set out the New Covenant and its God- provided benefits. We can then remedy the wrong in the charitable fashion of our Church's exclusive Eucharist. If the boys in Rome choose to stand obstinate, we, the People of God, can change their anti-Christ and uncharitable stance, perhaps by cutting off their funds. Together, we should establish the Church of Christ with a New Covenant law stating that Christ alone is our teacher. We should establish the new relationship between God and us in covenant, and we should establish the Kingdom of God that we inherited in its basic benefits. We should establish the actual Body of Christ to be impartially, openly, and lovingly shared in Eucharist, no strings attached. Thus, everyone comes to intimately be embraced by Our Almighty God, as He expected from the beginning of creation.

At its Second Vatican Council, the Roman Catholic Church acknowledged that the Church of Christ "subsists" in the Catholic Church. Sadly, since then Cardinal Ratzinger publicly said: "the true Church both is and can only be fully present in the Roman Catholic Church." Obviously, the Roman Catholic Church is not wholly and fully identified with the Church of Christ yet, and I express this concern to the People of God in the world who make up the body of the Church of Christ. Since the Catholic Church differs from the Church of Christ, I refer to them the need for fraternal correction of the Church. To date, the thrust of my writings has been aimed at the Roman Catholic Church's lack of the fundamental Christian virtue of charity when denying the people of the Church of Christ our Holy Communion.

I suspect that the oppressive silence I experience from my spiritual leaders is not solely arrogance lording over me, but it constitutes indifference to my concerns. However, their silence to my contentions may imply that I am correct. In evaluating evidence from silence in my trials, judges instructed jurors in the common law, as follows:

> If you find that . . . a party failed to reply . . . to a statement concerning his conduct . . . that he heard and understood . . . that he had a reasonable opportunity to reply . . . that he was in such . . . condition that he reasonably could reply, and . . . the statement was made under circumstances that it would normally call for an answer, you may then consider whether his . . . conduct indicated that he adopted the statement or believed it to be true.

Therefore, I choose to assume my leader's admissions from their respective silence, but I also want them to admit the truths to the world. So, assuming Pope Benedict agrees with the obvious, that

God's pledges to Jeremiah of making a New Covenant in coming days occurred in Jesus shedding the Blood of the Covenant on Calvary, then God's greatest Covenant since creation is being wrongly ignored. The Jewish people, as well as the Christians, silenced both Prophets Jesus and Jeremiah by following their consciences. Jews felt justified because they await another king like David or prophet like Moses, and not this criminal crucified on a tree to establish the New Covenant and New Kingdom. The New Covenant denial by Christians is not even conceded, and the justification for its negation escapes me. God made the promise of the New Covenant to Jeremiah 400 years before another prophet, Jesus, extended the Covenant to all humanity by shedding His blood, the blood of the covenant. Paul of Tarsus recorded the best evidence in history that God delivered on His covenant to imprint in His people's hearts knowledge of Himself and His law to love everyone impartially. Another wise rabbi said the rest of our book of God's commandment of love is commentary to it. Thus, Mahatma Ghandi liked Christianity and would have appreciated the New Covenant despite disliking the colonial Christians he witnessed practicing the variation of Christianity that lacks the Covenant. The people of Islam, also of the book, are forgiven of their evildoings, as are Jews and all Gentiles. By their God's goodness in unilaterally performing the New Covenant, upon the shedding of the blood of the prophet acknowledged to be Jesus, and with the sharing Eucharist, God may renew Islam. Jesus' last words were that He sheds the blood of the Covenant to ransom the world from everlasting death, and we all are ordered to take the cup in submission to this truth and be thankful to God for continuing to redeem us.

Jesus, according to Paul, "did not deem equality with God something to be grasped at. Rather, he emptied himself and took the form of a slave, being born in the likeness of men . . . he humbled himself, obediently accepting even death, death on a cross!" Consequently, God mysteriously uses Jesus as His agent, instrument, Son, and self to intimately relate with the entire human race. Believing Jesus is God seems to not literally be essential to the New Covenant form of Christianity, in which God forgives us for our evildoing and teaches us what we need to know. Simply stated, even if people do not consider Jesus divine, God still loves them as they are. Jesus' demonstration proves God's love and shows how we are to love God. God also will take into consideration one's love of Jesus as God, love of Jesus as man, or love of Jesus as mystery God man. For in the hereafter, there is judgment to reward or mitigate chastisements based on the extent, if any, that one believes in Christ as Lord.

Imagine this: a funeral for a non-Catholic American businessman, something we may have experienced. The man was considered good, yet paid no attention to God or Christ. I remember a specific event like that. It was for a man probably better than most. He was a real property salesman but unique in that he truly was honest. He succeeded in his occupation because he was skillful but even moreso because of his honesty. His interests were more in making a good deal than in the commission he would earn. Although his ethics and morals were of the highest order, his burial ritual was nonreligious. The speakers heartily spoke well of him for his lifetime of rags to riches success and for sharing it with his community and those less able, but they spoke with little mention of God. The songs played fit him, for example: "I had to be free . . . I had to be me . . .," Frank Sinatra's "when in doubt . . . I had myself . . .," and "I'll do it my way." All pleased God, who the deceased may never have acknowledged except for appreciating that God left him alone to pursue and enjoy life. In turn, he respectfully let God be God. Probably to appease some family member, we also heard, "Amazing Grace . . . that saved a wretch like me . . .," a truth the property salesman likely appreciated in Our Lord's company as we listened to the Christian hymn for him. But our deceased did not believe in Christ as God, and most Catholics would think him damned if they believed in what is written in Ch. II of *Lumen Gentium*. However, as an entrepreneur dealing in contracts, the deceased would appreciate the unilateral performance of the Covenant by our Creator and be thankful, had he known to hold his Creator to the deal. Jesus would be appreciated as an agent of this unknown covenant maker. He was authorized to fulfill the terms of the Covenant by paying and delivering a performance on the promised terms. All his life this man was raised among Protestants by his family and our enlightened culture, thus he was biased against the Papacy and any Catholic rule over him. He might have pointed out that Rome's emperor dressed in red shoes and parades in silly clothes, while no Catholic dare mention our emperor's dress. He would especially resent Pope Benedict XVI withholding the gift of the Eucharist purchased by Jesus, an edict based on Benedict's uncharitable translation of a couple of questionable bible passages that contradict a school of New Testament scholars' translation. He would be personally offended by the gift being withheld from him by a self-interested Roman Catholic hierarchy's clinging to human tradition through distorting the terms of the aforesaid Covenant and violating simple rules of common law justice as well as a God-given right to possess this gift of love from Him. However, he was never confronted with these wrongs done to him, and he rests in peace because he was unaffiliated with any particular religious group or faith, keeping him from appreciating his loss. He rarely was vocal about his non-belief and so remained comfortable in the society of Christians, Atheists, believers, and nonbelievers. He favored those who allowed him to be himself in mutual respect, including God as described above. He died a reputed good man and was likely welcomed by Jesus Christ for a life well done. He was simply a product of God's New Covenant, a Covenant Christ recreated. However, the tragedy of his life was the fact that he did not meet the Real Presence of Christ at our Lord's Supper. Thereby, both he and Our Lord lost out. His invitations to thank, praise, bless, know, love, and serve the Lord at Jesus' table were never received and were likely barred by the Church's traditional exclusions and uncharitable Eucharist. It is a loss to both God and humanity. Religions nullified Christ's message by negating evidence of the New Covenant fulfilled in the blood sacrifice of Christ.

The image of the entrepreneur that I described was a close friend of mine. Had he been aware of God's saving action in history, he would have appreciated God's New Covenant terms gained in Jesus' fatal purchase, and he would have likely gained a better reception in the hereafter. The love defined by Jesus in doing the will of his Respondeat Superior is a love my friend practiced all his life in honest dealings, doing the will of God. Much of his negotiations were in mutual trust. Thus, the idea of the Eucharist would appeal to him, and we should credit Our Lord with great wisdom in instituting this method of exchange as part of his continuing redemptive action in human history. Readers may ask why I did not bring my faith to my friend's awareness. I am reluctant to teach the world my thoughts as it presumes on the space Our Lord retains to teach, and I write with that same reluctance. Had *Lumen Gentium* not burdened me with the obligation, I doubt that you or the Church of Christ would be troubled with my thinking. I figured that God has set the pattern in the New Covenant and may even prohibit the teachings of others. The Lord alone teaches us to live life as my friend lived his life, fully and happily, and God takes care of teaching and forgiving him. Knowing of my reluctance to speak of my faith convictions, especially to a friend, I figure is why God prefers to do it all Himself. Besides, I believe my friend learned what God wished to teach him. God knows us as we are, and God knows when He should take over the task of teaching. But, inept as I am, I have been allowed to write. I wish I could tell everyone sooner and better about the Eucharist; however, I hope those who read my writings learn whatever God wants to teach by them. I suggest people live and let live in imitation of Jesus Christ's Covenant and my departed friend's life story.

Non practicing Paulist Priest James Carroll wrote in <u>Practicing Catholic</u> his recollection of seminary days watching Pope John XXIII and his assembled bishops on T.V., discussing assiduously point after point, of the Second Vatican Council. He reports the seminarian's studied conclusions: (1) religion was about revelation not salvation; (2) revelation that we all are already saved; and, (3) God loves us simply because we are being or becoming as God created us. Carroll's life story exemplifies how God teaches us all in hearts and minds. Even Jesus, while emptied of divinity, wanted us to gift God with our things and love. Thus, God gave us the Eucharist mainly to thank God. My above-mentioned non-practicing religious friend now knows what he missed in life of my Church withholding Eucharist from him.

Speaking for myself again, I obediently try to follow the teachings of Christ, as I understand them in their more charitable translations. I am dedicated to the idea of the Roman Catholic Church's Eucharist being God's gift to everyone. I, like Ambrose, frequently go to Holy Communion because I sin a lot, but mostly because I trust Jesus at His word, "Take this, all of you . . . ." I could not consider a rebellion or disobedience against my Catholic Church that would jeopardize my access to the Eucharist. However, I would consider disobedience in not following or imitating the example of my Catholic hierarchy in order to obey the words and teachings of Jesus Christ, which I ought to do because Jesus trustfully said "Only one is our teacher, the Messiah." All of you readers, who agree or disagree with me, follow your own Christ informed consciences, but also trust Jesus by taking Communion. Come at Jesus' open invitation to his table to consume his Real Presence, especially when you never met Him there or are buried in vice or evildoing, and trust Him to renew God in your redemption. You, who hesitate, still try it your way. I bet our Lord will be pleased whether or not you try to please God or choose to reject Him, as you would have momentarily paid attention and not been indifferent to God. Try coming to Holy Communion; you will enjoy it someday because God, like my entrepreneur friend, returns favors. In life, you may have given yourself the feeling of God's goodness that is lacking in taking or receiving. However, any effort in taking or receiving the Eucharist is an experience of God that essentially comes from trusting Jesus' order: "take this!" It is about trusting Almighty God, who hereby stoops to embrace each and every one of us in His mysterious Eucharist and Covenant. So, enjoy your thanksgiving with God. He will intimately embrace you at His breast and make your Communion One with Him in His Pleasure.

What I have tried to tell you is obviously my view and faith convictions and perhaps not anything that you do not already know in your hearts and minds. I write about these matters shortly after my daily practice of consuming the Eucharist. It is a way for me to get informed that I have much experienced, but I cannot prove it is an inspiration. I trust that Christ will remedy any wrong I cause you in my communication of these faith convictions, which I hope involve the Spirit of God. I have added some prayers that I use after consuming the Divine meal. Use any that you feel fits your grateful accepting of Christ's invitation to receive the Eucharist. I share the following thoughts and prayers that I usually use to try to more fully experience the Real Presence in Holy Communion, not that I can vouch for any success in them, but they comfort me at that moment of trying to embrace the Lord within me.

Just as I trust that God imprints in everyone's conscience how to know Him and His law of love, God, through Christ, invites or orders everyone to consume His Real Presence in the Eucharist. So, no matter your faith or conviction of mind, God Himself may transform you to better hear Christ's story firsthand, and by consuming his body and blood in the form of bread and wine, you will experience God on earth as He wants you to do. Trust God in this, just as you may trust that you do not die into nothingness, but into Godliness forever.

If you say "yes" to the invitation from Jesus to "Take this, all of you, and eat it," or "Take this, all of you, and drink from it" in Communion, you trust the meaningfulness of God being active in human history. Just as you may assume you likely will not die into nothingness, but into Godliness, the presence of God is presumed to meet you in Communion. God is actually in Real Presence in both experiences. Your experience of God's presence is based upon the awareness and appreciation that God graces you with at the moment. Those such as I, who have been conditioned with a life of faith convictions in God's presence, accept God's real presence not on basis of rational perception or reasoning, but on basis of an absolutely reasonable trust in God and His words.

At daily Mass, immediately after receipt of the body and blood of Jesus Christ in form of bread and wine, I reflect on what may be happening within me by first viewing a crucifix that is located above our altar. I imagine that I see Christ in this crucifix reminder, at rest as he has died.

> **Lo, there he hangs —**
> **ashen figure pinioned**
> **against the wood.**
> **God grant that**
> **I might love Him**
> **even as I should**
> **I draw a little closer**
> **To feel His love**
> **divine,**

and hear Him
gently whisper,
"Ah, precious child
Of mine . . ."

Assuming a whisper that I really imagine comes from the Real Presence that I have consumed within me, I change my focus from the crucifix to my interior and pray from a card in my missal:

Loving God, please awaken in me an awareness and appreciation of Your interior presence. Invite me to be drawn to meet You.

Help me to initially consider thoughts of Jesus loving Us: beginning with his scriptural life, baptism, journey to Jerusalem, Last Supper, Gethsemane, scourging, crowning, way of cross, crucifixion and death.

Keep me detached except, focusing on the love shown by Jesus and on Your response, to awaken thanksgiving and reciprocal love in me.

Finally, I try to finish praying the following, from another card, before announcements or the end of Mass distract me:

O Jesus, I adore you and I praise you. By dying on the cross, you have redeemed the world. By your precious body and blood you have cleansed my soul. O dear Jesus, how great is your love! I pray that some day I will be worthy to enjoy eternal happiness with you forever in heaven. Amen.

What follows beyond this point in this published Sequel is similar to the format I had in *God's Gift To You* (available online: Trafford. com/07–0459 or Library of Congress database LCCN #2007373670). I have attached copies of letters from between April 2008 and April 2009 mailed to my spiritual shepherds: Pope Benedict, diocesan bishops Wiegand and Soto, and parish pastor, Francisco Hernandez.

———————————————

April 14, 2008

His Holiness Pope Benedict XVI
Apostolic Palace
00120 Vatican City State
Europe

Dear Holy Father,

Today, we heard "what God has purified you are not to call unclean" (Acts 11:9). Yet the Church's Eucharist excludes many unclean or unreconciled people, as you suggested we do in *God Is Near Us*. Therein, you contradicted the post-Vatican II New Testament scholars' contention that Christ invited everyone to the Lord's Supper. In your doctoral dissertation of Donatism, you knew the risk of not being "true church" because of sacramental exclusion. In 1968/9, you also lectured that Jesus linked himself to the "new covenant" performance on behalf "of many" (Mk 14:24), preventing a discriminating selection of only righteous Catholics in favor of the many (*Commonweal*, 4/21/06). At the same period, you preached that the death of Jesus, which redeemed everyone, was "interdependent" with the words of the Last Supper. Those words, charitably translated, invited everyone.

At Mass, the sacrifice of the Cross and Eucharist are all of one-piece. God's Redemption continues to save everyone, regardless of time and space. Today, we hear the liturgy's divine cleansing of everyone, and we hear the Consecration on "behalf of many," referring to all humanity. Thus, limiting the Church's Eucharist for only graceful Catholics is wrong and merits Jesus' insult (Mk 7:6-8).

So long as you, Pope Benedict XVI, allow the Catholic Church to deny "the many" God's gift, the Church of Christ does not subsist in the Catholic Church. You should be concerned about not recognizing the body of the Church of Christ (1 Cor 11:29).

Yours in Christ,

FRED B.
ITHURBURN

cc: Most Rev. Jaime Soto
        Rev. Francisco Hernandez
        Rev. Donald Senior, C.P.

April 18, 2008

Dear Holy Father,

I wondered why President Bush thanked you for the global example he sees you setting. Likely unknown to Bush was your visit to Brazil in 2007 and your exemplary address. On the issue of globalization as benefiting "the great family of humanity and [being] a sign of its profound aspiration toward unity," you insisted that it "must be led by ethics, placing everything at the service of the human person, created in the image and likeness of God." Other than this address, Bush had some altruism in mind. The Church's Eucharist that concerns me would not be of as much interest to Bush as global altruism.

Vatican II established a global Church of Christ from its ressourcement of Christ's words at the Last Supper. You contradicted the New Testament scholars' contention that Christ placed the Eucharist at the service of every human being, regardless of denomination or state of sin. Your contradicting opinion (*God Is Near Us*, pp. 59-60) caused the Catholic Church's Eucharist to exclude most humans from the service. It was not globally loving or devoted to the welfare of others, except for select Catholics.

It remains beyond my understanding why you champion the Church's Eucharist, because I read prior inconsistent ideas from you. For example, you preached the following: (1) Jesus' death and last words were "interdependent," giving meaning to his death (and arguably a universal communion [*Infra*, p. 29]); (2) Jesus' death sealed the Covenant to bring us all into "a communion of God and man" (*Infra*, p. 39); and (3) Christ, fully present in Eucharist, "we can only receive him together with everyone else" (*Infra*, p. 52). Thus, the Eucharist that you found tempting, as described in 1968 by the New Testament scholars, was consistent with your own prior contentions. Had you listened to your heart, I too would thank you for the global example you set in supporting the Church of Christ as described in *Lumen Gentuim*, fulfilling the Eucharist in love for God and our neighbor.

A *Commonweal*, 4/11/08, book review by Orthodox Father John Garvey seems to agree with your more charitable ideas. He writes "in a creation redeemed and perfected, the world as God finally means it to be, communion and otherness coexist as they do in the Trinity." The article commented on the global situation because of "the inadequacy of ethics where love of others is concerned," which seems fitting to our criticism of the Church's Eucharist being ethically discriminate.

Unlike Bush, I take issue with the global example you and my Catholic Church set in excluding most of our human family from the Church's Eucharist. It is unethical, uncharitable and not Christ's Eucharist, in my humble analysis. In "obedience of faith" to Christ, I criticize the Church's Eucharist.

Yours concernedly,

April 23, 2008

Dear Holy Father,

You presided spectacularly at Mass, repeating the words of Jesus Christ, "this is my body which will be given up for you," and "this is the cup of my blood the blood of the new and everlasting covenant. It will be shed for you and for all so that sins may be forgiven. Do this in memory of me." Jesus' sacrifice and yours at Mass were of one-piece, in time and space; even though you spoke in the USA and in the future tense. St. Augustine taught you that the passages should be translated from the standard of LOVE, including universal love towards all humanity. You appreciated that God performs, through Jesus Christ, the pledge He made with all mankind (Jer 31) in these words and acts, redeeming everyone and teaching them to know, love, and serve God.

By means of the sacrifice of the Cross and the Sacrament of Eucharist, through you God imprinted LOVE on hearts as sins were forgiven and forgotten throughout the world. Participants may reciprocate from this show, but their transformation by memory of Christ or God's actual presence within them was denied, and it denied many to live as God lives. The experience of love the way God loves us was given to a few Communicants, while the remainder were left to live their lives as outsiders of God's Kingdom.

On TV, many of us more knowledgeable plainly saw the scandal of the Church's Eucharist as you all discriminately distributed Christ's actual presence to only select Catholics. The Divine Gift of God was given to cling to human Catholic tradition, disregarding God's commandment of love of neighbor. For one-fourth of an hour, the Heavenly Food was given only to those who you, mainly you, felt were worthy of nourishment. The world witnessed God's sacrifice at Calvary, but it saw Christ petered out in a meal to cleanse only Church-cleansed Catholics. Not only was Christ's universal sacrifice for the many wasted on a travesty, but you proved to the world that our Eucharist is not an all-loving event meant by God to demonstrate His continuing Redemption of the new covenant. Jesus prophesied the hierarchy's hypocrisy in Mark 7:1-13, where people pay heartless lip service to God and neighbor in "obedience of faith" to Church.

I suspect that you know better than my diocesan bishop the extent to which the Church's Eucharist practice disregards the Christian sense of love. You have the time and ability to remedy the Church's wrongdoing so that the Eucharist will be as Jesus Christ ordered, with everyone taking it in order to please God. It is a Divine Eucharist to be given to everyone so God may transform all to know, love, and serve Him as He intended. Bluntly, the goodness of God dictates that everyone is equally worthy to receive the body and blood of Christ.

Yours in Christ,

_____

Fred Ithurburn

May 1, 2008

Father Pat McCloskey, O.F.M.
Ask a Franciscan
28 W. Liberty Street
Cincinnati, OH 45202-6498

Dear Father Pat,

The reverse of this page is a Xerox copy of pages from Joseph Cardinal Ratzinger's *God Is Near Us*. The pages contradict our New Testament scholars' post-Vatican II idea of having a universal Eucharist.

Your advice to a couple in the *St. Anthony Messenger* of 5/08 seems to be appropriate advice to send Pope Benedict XVI. You wrote, in part, as follows:

> Is God so fragile that the Almighty needs your help . . .
> to prevent people not properly disposed from receiving
> Holy Communion? This issue is on that person's
> conscience—not on yours.

The problem in denying the Eucharist from most everyone but disposed Catholics puts this issue on our spiritual leaders' conscience. They should be warned that they may not be recognizing that the body of Christ includes all non-disposed sinners when doing the charitable act.

Sincerely,

FRED B.
ITHURBURN

cc: His Holiness Pope Benedict XVI
        Most Revs. Wm. Wiegand and Jaime Soto

———————————

presented with the *essential element*, but it has not yet found a new Christian form. Not until the moment when, through the Cross and the Resurrection and the story that followed, the Church emerged from within Israel as an independent community could this new gift find its own new form. And that gives rise to the question: From what source did the Mass actually derive its shape, if it was not possible to repeat the entire Last Supper as such? What could the disciples build upon to develop this new shape?

✱ Nowadays New Testament scholars essentially give one of two answers. Some of them say that the Eucharist of the early Church built upon meals that Jesus shared with his disciples day after day. Others say that the Eucharist is the *continuation of the meals with sinners* that Jesus had held.[2] This second idea has become for many people a fascinating notion with far-reaching consequences. For it would mean that the Eucharist is the sinners' banquet, where Jesus sits at the table; the Eucharist is the public gesture by which he invites everyone without exception. The logic of this is expressed in a far-reaching criticism of the Church's Eucharist, since it implies that the Eucharist cannot be conditional on anything, not dependent on denomination or even on baptism. It is necessarily an open table to which all may come to encounter the universal God, without any limit or denominational preconditions. But then, again—however tempting the idea may be—it contradicts what we find in the Bible. Jesus' Last Supper was not one of those meals he held with "publicans and sinners". He made it subject to the basic form of the Passover, which implies that this meal was held in a family setting.

✱Emphasis mine

[2] There are more details on this in my essay, "Gestalt und Gehalt der eucharistischen Feier" [Form and content in the eucharistic celebration], in my *Das Fest des Glaubens*, 3d ed. (Einsiedeln, 1993), pp. 31–54 [English trans., *The Feast of Faith*, trans. Graham Harrison (San Francisco: Ignatius Press, 1986), pp. 33–60].

May 7, 2008

Dear Holy Father,

I think there is a parallel between denying life to Jews for being "Christ Killers" and denying everlasting life in Eucharist to non-Catholics because they are not disposed Catholics. You have been part of both denials, the first as a Hitler youth and the second, starting in 1968 to the present date, in pressing your idea of a Eucharist for select Catholics only. A survivor of Auschwitz, Primo Levi, wrote *"If Not Now, When?"* This title impacts on your duty of love. Your duty is to extend the blessing of Christ's Eucharist to Levi and those who you deem unworthy to share the Lord's Supper.

I am sure that long ago you became aware that the Holocaust was wrong, but I am unable to determine the truth of your thinking on the Church's Eucharist. Pages 59 and 60 in *God Is Near Us* give questionable clues to what you thought in 1968, such as: (1) there were "far reaching consequences" where Jesus invites everyone to an open table, but you left us wondering what consequences; and (2) "it contradicts what we find in the Bible." I don't know who "we" are, but I doubt if "we" have any greater expertise or impartiality than the New Testament scholars whom you contradict. At worst, you demonstrate incompetence in citing Jn 13:10, 1 Cor 11, and in misciting *Didache* 10:6 to support your own opinion. Besides uncharity, I would charge you as simply incorrect in your analysis, and I assert that you need "obedience of faith" to Christ's teaching. The only "far reaching consequence" apparent to me is that Christ blesses those who share Eucharist. Why not love now?

Since attaining your present status, you have never made the Church's Eucharist a matter of dogma. You delegated this matter to diocesan bishops for final judgment. This persuades me to think that you are wary of outright denying the body of Christ to anyone. More ignorant diocesan bishops are delegated this risk. God made holy what the Church again deems sinful. Bishops follow your uncharitable opinion and nullify God's word (Mk 7:1-13). God commands you to love everyone equally.

St. Augustine instructed you to translate the Bible by the standard of love for neighbor. You even wrote of his contention to deny Donatism as true Church for uncharitably denying sacraments. These thoughts you possess convince me that you, as Pope, constitute God's best remedy to the wrong of our Eucharist's denial to anyone. You best know why and how to love.

However, neither you nor any of your hierarchy chooses open hearts or minds to discuss this matter with me—to show me where, if anywhere, my analysis is incorrect. *Lumen Gentium* prevents me from remaining silent on a matter that concerns the good of the Church. A blind "obedience of faith" to accept the teaching of the Church is the only alternative you all leave me. I owe more than that to my LORD, Jesus Christ, and it seemingly is my cross to bear without the hoped for dialogue provided in paragraph 37 of our Dogmatic Constitution on the Church. Let us love and at least correspond.

Yours in Christ,

_____

May 12, 2008

Dear Holy Father,

God in me may be talking to God in you. You won't listen, but I must speak.

You once preached that the words which instituted the Eucharist in anticipation of Christ's death shape the mystery of Christ in proving the truth of his love. Thereby, Christ shares Himself in his death *into the act of self-sharing love* to God. Then, from God He is made available to men. The death and words constitute this event, which Christ meant for us to regard as constantly guaranteed by the pledge of his blood

(*God Is Near Us*, pp. 29-30). But your Church's Eucharist speaks to the contrary and nullifies Christ's event for many who will never share Christ in his way.

From you, we learned that the blood of the new and everlasting covenant, something constantly shed for us in the memorial sacrifice of our everyday Eucharist, is from Christ's words of Redemption to fulfill God's pledge (Jer 31). Your transcribed lecture notes acknowledge the Last Supper words as explanation of the "new covenant" in Mk 14:24, and those words prevent the church from selecting less than all and "condemn[ing] the wayward masses to perdition" (*Commonweal*, 4/21/06). But your Eucharist denies God's redemption effect to most everyone.

Your teachings show you lack *caritas* when you culpably practice the Church's Eucharist today. After Vatican II, you admitted to being confronted with the theologians and New Testament scholars' faith convictions that dictate that Christ meant for a universal Communion. Your edited sermons in *God Is Near Us* at pages 59-60 are evidence for your reversal of heart. As Pope, your Vatican has since then artfully used the Synod and *Sacramentum Caritatis* to revive the pre-Vatican II Church's Eucharist based on its centuries of tradition. But, I feel that you wish you had the moral courage to do what you ought to do—rule for a universal Eucharist.

On April 18th, you addressed the UN General Assembly and emphasized their duty to uphold human rights. Drawing on John XXIII, you told them he taught that our failure to protect against violations of people's rights makes governing bodies illegitimate. Long ago, you wrote the same thing in your doctoral dissertation on your mentor St. Augustine's teaching that Donatism was not true Church for denying sacramental rights to people who had such rights by God's command of love. So, how can you, as Pope Benedict XVI, personally discriminate against the rights of the "wayward masses" you mention above by continuing to deny Holy Communion to all but select Catholics? Only by *Maxima Culpa* on your part can you allow the Church's Eucharist to discriminate.

Concernedly yours,

―――――――――――――

May 13, 2008

Dear Holy Father,

Each Wednesday morning, I try to receive Holy Communion with the faith conviction that the blood I receive is Christ's blood of the new covenant (Jer 31, Lk 22:20, Mt 26:28, Mk 14:24, and 1 Cor 11:25).

Thus, I experience the words of the Last Supper and Jesus' death on the Cross as the same event in the time and space of Christ's continuing redemption and forgiveness of my faults, imprinting on my heart and mind the knowledge of God and God's law of love. Whatever transforming effect I receive at Mass, I carry it for a time to share with the less fortunate.

Within the hour, I am trying to relate what I have received to a Bible study group made up of the homeless who attend our local Baptist Rescue Mission. Recidivists, felons, addicts, and poor people of many faiths come and go during these study sessions of the New Testament. Many continue to believe Catholics are not Christian, and others accuse my discernments of being Satan-inspired. We struggle to understand, but we have persevered for years in our exchanges. I think God is pleased.

I have experienced some moments when a few of us have a meeting of minds or hearts. Some have shown this interest after reading of the new covenant pledges by God extended to them by Jesus' Last Supper words. They enjoy those same words, the words explaining that they all are saved on the merits of Jesus alone. The wonder of Jesus saving them, "taking the rap" for them while they sin, brings them peace of mind. They add to this satisfaction that Christ alone is their teacher, imprinting in their minds and hearts whatever lasting knowledge God expects them to know. God loves them just as they are. They carry that joy with them no matter what life has dealt.

Still, these few moments of grace are not what God meant for them to have as Eucharist. God meant for the Church to use Christ, in the flesh and intimately consumed, to transform the lives and faiths of all created people. Can you not see this? The New Testament scholars, after Vatican II, saw and confronted you with this, but you succeeded in silencing them and in denying most sinners Christ in Eucharist.

Concernedly yours,

_____

May 20, 2008

Dear Holy Father,

Wednesday, I read my letter from 5/13/08 to my Bible study group at the Baptist Rescue Mission. On this occasion, we studied that portion of John's Gospel that states we will be lifeless if we "do not eat the flesh of the Son of God." Fr. Daniel Harrington, S.J. says this includes eternally participating with God in the life of Jesus (America, 5/19/08). I received Holy Communion that morning, about one hour before, and expressed hope to them that Christ in the flesh within me might assist our studies. We hoped that the actual Christ in me participating with Christ in them would be conducive for God transforming our faiths and lives.

One listener informed us that he frequented Holy Communion as a child. Since then, he has been in prison and has attended other churches, the most recent of which preached that all Catholics go to hell. During our exchange, it dawned on the both of us that we were acquainted in his youth. He conceded that, like me, he struggled with the dictates of his conscience. Today, I feel guilty in not inviting him to return to share our Eucharist. The Catholic in me would suggest that he needed to confess his sins before doing so. Christ, however, had no such requisite, and He probably expected more of me and all of you — to invite everyone unconditionally.

I believe that you should share any guilt from my failing to invite him, because you returned Christ's Eucharist back to the traditional perversion, exclusively practicing for reconciling Catholics for centuries.

In 1968/9, had you agreed with the New Testament scholars' ideal for an open, unconditional invitation to everyone, my fall-away Catholic acquaintance might again participate at Christ's or the Church's invitation. You still can remedy any wrongdoing on your part by giving back to these strayed sheep what Christ gave them with no strings attached. Why do you not do as Christ does or, at least, as Christ orders you? Feed his sheep.

Yours in Christ,

_____

May 23, 2008

America
106 West 56th Street
New York, NY 10019-3803

Dear Editor,

In your 5/26/08 edition, Fr. Robert F. Taft, S.J. wrote this Eucharistic theology, "The dynamic of the Eucharist is one continuous movement, in which the community gifts are offered, accepted by God and returned to the community to be shared as God's gift to us, a sharing of something we receive from God and give to one another—in short, a communion."

The identical dynamic of the sacrifice in Mass is one piece, in time and space, with the sacrifice of Christ on Calvary. Christ Himself is our community gift, returned to us by God, to be shared from God with one another in Holy Communion.

In 1968/9, Fr. Joseph Ratzinger opposed our New Testament scholars' contention for an open Communion, including everyone as recipients of God's gift. Today, we have returned to the dynamic of our traditional Church's Communion, which denies God's gift to many. The Catholic Church opts for tradition over love of neighbor—love of the many.

Yours in Christ
FRED B.
ITHURBURN

cc: His Holiness Pope Benedict XVI
      Most Revs William Wiegand and Jaime Soto

May 28, 2008

Dear Holy Father,

I feel fortunate for my passionate involvement in expressing my opinion on behalf of a catholic Eucharist. My concern for the subject has become a discovered pearl for which I willingly sacrifice much to pass it on to my Catholic Church. I likely will not succeed in my solo efforts, but I believe the futile attempts please God moreso than any accomplishment I have made in life.

Among the more than 160 letters I published in *God's Gift To You*, at page 120, I commented on Scott Hahn's *A Father Who Keeps his Promises* about his reference to the New Covenant's fulfillment by Jesus Christ on the Cross. He wrote of everyone being family "with the Eucharist serving as the sign of the New Covenant, making God's family truly <u>universal</u> (<u>katholikos</u> in Greek), otherwise known as the <u>Catholic Church</u>." By the New Covenant, Hahn writes "all human beings are called to become members of this universal family of God in order to serve as instruments in the Father's work of reconciliation through the Son and by the Spirit. Human power alone is incapable to such task" (34-35). Hahn agrees with me that humanity is family.

Dr. Hahn, a convert, in effect also agrees with Joseph Cardinal Ratzinger's opinions on page 29 of his edited sermons in *God Is Near Us*. Hahn writes that "Jesus seals the New Covenant with us through his self offering. This sacrifice began in the Upper Room . . ." and he later adds about Christ's sacrifice on Calvary, "It is all of one piece." But, Hahn also points out that the Eucharistic is, in fact, one and the same sacrifice as Jesus' sacrificial death, but it does not end there, "Since the main purpose is to restore communion, we have to eat the Lamb" (242 and 237). I entirely agree with Hahn that Mass is one piece with the Cross.

God pledged in the New Covenant that "from least to greatest" (Jer 31:34) we now know God, God's law to love, and our duty to serve everyone as equals. So, there is no need for me to teach my spiritual shepherds what they already know. Everyone on earth should be invited to Mass and Eucharist. Everyone created is meant to be at the foot of the Cross to proclaim God's goodness and love of us in a communion that makes us Christ and Catholic throughout time and space.

Both the greatest of us enthroned in Rome and the least of us writing this letter know that loving neighbors as ourselves mandates sharing a catholic Communion. Jesus complained, "You disregard God's commandment and cling to what is human tradition," in respect to dining with people with dirty hands (Mk 7:1-13). Knowing better, Peter need not hear again from God, "that no one should call any man unclean or impure" (Acts 10:28). Knowing better, please, do it for Christ's sake!

Yours in Christ,

_____

Dear Holy Father,

Sunday, June 1st, I read Deuteronomy 11:18-32 as lecturer. It was meant to transform Moses' people from the inside out to be God's holy nation by means of law within them. We, at Mass, are there to be transformed in faith and life by receipt of Christ in Holy Communion, and, by Christ within us, we all expand into one holy people that God desires us to be.

The fact that you once interpreted the Bible to imply that the Lord's Supper was to be narrowly held to a family setting made up of only Roman Catholics surprised me. Before Vatican II, we experienced that traditional form of Eucharist, keeping with our bias for only Catholics, instead of everyone. In rebuttal of the New Testament scholars' contentions for a universal Communion, you preached your Catholics only presupposition in 1968/9. Your continuing support of the absurdity of an uncharitable Communion, denying Christ to so many, astonishes me. Of course, I assume that you are aware of enough of my correspondence to suspect the risk of your way. I argue thus because I know that you are far from being a fool, but as you approach that judgment day before Christ, I submit that you are foolish to persist in maintaining your Church's Eucharistic exclusions. To deliberately exclude most of God's people from His plan for all human beings is brazenly foolhardy when considering scripture of God's law to love your neighbor as one people. Christ soon may ask why you denied Him nourishment.

Why don't you engage in "Pascal's wager"? Hedge the bet that you are correct in supporting the Church's Eucharist by having all diocesan bishops open their hearts and their Lord's Supper to invite everyone as though they were all God's people. If we are wrong in doing so, it is better strategy to love and err than to wager all on your skill as a scriptural scholar or on your self righteousness.

By copy of this letter, I am addressing my diocesan bishop in the same way, because he too can easily remedy the wrongdoing by use of his empowered authority from *Sacramentum Caritatis*. May he be graced to do God's will, rather than copy yours.

Yours in Christ,

_____

June 9, 2008

Dear Holy Father,

The 5/30/06 edition of *NCR* reports that because Archbishop John N. Nienstedt believes the ordained has been empowered to sacred service, "There is the power of the Holy Spirit that goes with him that doesn't go to just anyone who has been baptized."

Assuming the above to be true, I, a baptized person, plead with you, the ordained, to consider my concerns about the Church's Eucharist. With the power, you have greater duties to serve Holy Communion to everyone that God meant to be redeemed by Jesus Christ.

As a lawyer, I note the inconsistencies between ordained witnesses on the issue. The New Testament scholars in 1968/9 agreed with my concerns about the Church's Eucharist, and they contended that Christ meant for the Eucharist to be open to all sinners as part of God's plan. You, on the other hand, publicly preached an exclusive Eucharist for select Catholics based mostly on your subjective presuppositions.

In 1968/9, your typescript lecture notes linked Christ's words at the Last Supper, fulfilling God's pledges in the New Covenant (Jer 3), to explain his sacrificial death on the Cross. You even preached that those words were "interdependent" with Christ's death. You taught that the Eucharistic blood, "which is being shed for many" (Mk 14:24), prevented the Church from favoring a select community of the righteous, prejudiced to the masses. By implication, you taught and preached inconsistently to dispute your exclusive Eucharist's validity.

The New Covenant itself is a fact obvious to any competent lawyer—a unilateral agreement whereby God pledges to perform its provisions without human contribution, except for the participation of Christ. Christ's words and death forgive all evil that men commit. Christ alone, by word and act, teaches us that God loves us even while we do evil. God loves us as we are.

Thus, the Holy Spirit teaches Bible toting recidivist sinners imprisoned in San Quentin to claim that the Blood of the Lamb saves them, no matter what they do. Father Dennis Burke, Chaplain at the prison, reported his concern and frustration (*Commonweal*, 12/7/07). However, the felons are likely at peace and could use Eucharistic nourishment. Christ and the Eucharist proclaim liberty to captives. They proclaim mercy for sick sinners. They transform those habituated in sin to proclaim the death of Lord Jesus to each other, until he comes in glory. God wants to be with everyone *now*. A purpose of the Eucharist is to empower sinners to sacred service, a service disabled by you.

Concernedly yours,

_____

June 17, 2008

Dear Holy Father,

I mailed the message on the reverse page in a letter attached to my letter to you from 6/9/08.

Most of the thoughts I presented in both letters have your sermons and lectures in 1968/9 as their source. For instance:

1. Jesus' words of why he sheds "the blood of the new and everlasting covenant" refer to Jer 31:33-34 (your typescript lecture notes: *Commonweal*, 4/21/06). He is to perform the unilateral covenant, pledged by God, for all people, bar-none;

2. Jesus' words are "interdependent" with his death and gave it meaning (your book, *God Is Near Us*, p. 29); thus, by his acts God alone performs the covenant to redeem everyone, bar-none; and

3. Jesus' words "for many" (Mk 14:24) prevent redemption for only select, preferred Catholics (*Commonweal* 4/21/00) and means redemption for everyone, bar-none.

We both experienced post-Vatican II theologians and New Testament scholars' criticism of our traditional Eucharist and their 1964-1994 contentions that Christ meant for an open Eucharist to which all, including sinners and non-Catholics, were to be invited. Your edited sermon at page 59 and 60 of *God Is Near Us* recorded your 1968/9 argument. In opposition, you state, "—however tempting the idea may be—it contradicts what *we* find in the Bible" (Italics mine). The "we" is not identified and may refer to those traditionalists to whom you owe your elevations, perhaps by reason of your publicly voiced opinion. Circumstantially, Joseph Cardinal Ratzinger's innate self-interest appears by reason of the books' 2003 title page, showing your innate conservatism had apparently won out over time as you conceded a "we" group decision to the issue in controversy. Bluntly, an inference is that you "sold out" to the entrenched traditionalists in Rome.

Now that you are the Vicar of Christ and, presumably over with the ambitions, turmoil, and disputes of 1968/9, please apply *ressourcement* and reconsider doing Eucharist Christ's way, not the Church's traditional version with its lack of the fundamental Christian virtue of charity for all, bar-none. You best know of what I am talking about.

Concernedly yours,

_____

June 23, 2008

Dear Holy Father,

A thought came to me as we recited the first joyful mystery of the Rosary today. Mary, a teenaged virgin, was called on to decide to be impregnated in a society that would adversely judge her. To our salvation, she chose to do God's will.

The thought was of my spiritual shepherds' decision on a universal Eucharist. Sadly, one who knows better opposed the post-Vatican II New Testament scholars' contention that Christ intended a universal Eucharist, and he joined the traditionalist hierarchy to deny most of humanity what Christ died to institute. The other blindly followed his Pope's lead to deny Christ's access to would-be communicants in our diocese. Neither of the two risked an iota of what teenage Mary braved in order to do the will of God.

I hope the Holy Spirit reaches the heart or mind of either or both of you to urge you to obey God's law of love, instead of clinging to man-made traditions in respect of our Eucharist.

Yours in Christ,

_____

June 30, 2008

Dear Holy Father,

Jesus Christ's last words explained his death and the Eucharist in the context of God's new and everlasting Covenant, which reads, in part, as follows:

> But this is the covenant which I will make with the house of Israel after those days, says the LORD. I will place my law within them, and write it upon their

hearts, I will be their God and they shall be my people. No longer will they have need to teach their friends and kinsmen how to know the LORD. All, from least to greatest, shall know me says the LORD, for I will forgive their evildoing and remember their sin no more.

As a common law attorney, the covenant is obviously a unilateral agreement where God pledges to perform the whole deal. A bilateral one would be like a marriage contract, where both parties to the deal have obligations to fulfill. Through and by Jesus Christ, our sins are forgiven, and we know by heart that God is love, as demonstrated by Jesus' Eucharist and crucifixion. We are saved solely by God's gift to us.

Apparently, God's creation of man, with man's instinct for selfishness, was good, and God loved him as he created him. However, God wanted man to love Him, and Christ was the means to reveal God's love through his death—to obtain a reciprocal love from man in Christ's imitation. The sacrifice of Calvary was thusly memorialized in the Eucharist, so many would be aware of God's unilateral covenant of love and share it.

The New Testament scholars, who confronted you in 1968 with their claims that Christ meant for a universal Eucharist with natural sinning humans of every kind participating, manifested Vatican II's ressourcement. You argued that "it contradicts what we find in the Bible" (*God Is Near Us*, pp. 59 and 60) and thereafter "made a fine art of setting aside God's commandment in the interests of keeping your traditions!" (Mk 7:9). Both in translating scripture and in sharing Eucharist, love was wanting.

My diocesan bishop followed your example instead of that of Christ, our teacher (Mt 23:1-9). My bishop burdened us with Diocesan Statutes of human precepts, preventing non-Catholics and gravely sinning Catholics from receiving Holy Communion. He also wrote to me that I need "obedience of faith" to the teaching of the Church, and that I am simply incorrect in my analysis. I answer that you both need to love us.

I challenge either of you, or both of you, to publicly analyze this issue in order to know the will of Jesus Christ, Our LORD, which God Almighty's covenant imprinted in everyone's hearts and minds.

Yours in Christ,

_____

July 9, 2008

Dear Holy Father,

Pope Paul VI and his scribes promulgated *Lumen Gentium* to expressly state that the New Covenant of Jeremiah 31:31-34 was the one ratified by Christ in his Blood. But in actually quoting the Covenant, they distorted it by deleting God's pledge for why everyone will know him without needing a teacher other than Christ; to wit:

> . . . for I will forgive their evildoing and remember their sin no more. (Ch. II, No. 9)

The changing of the terms of the Covenant frees the Catholic Church to claim that God does not make men holy and save them merely as individuals; He only saves those who believe in Christ and the Church. It also justifies the Church's Eucharist in excluding those not reconciled to the Church. However, Jesus and Isaiah critically prophesied about such experts of the law not loving everyone equally (Mk 7:1-13).

Dr. Scott Hahn, a scriptural scholar and convert (I referred to him in my letter to you from 12/27/06), agreed with your astute conviction that the words of the Last Supper were "interdependent" with Christ's death. Hahn writes "Eucharist is also inseparably united to Jesus' death . . . In fact, they are one and the same sacrifice!" (*A Father Who Keeps His Promises,* p. 234). He concluded so while a protestant professor, but he learned that it was so taught by the *Baltimore Catechism.* As a Catholic, he wrote, "the sixth covenant was made by <u>Jesus Christ</u>, with the Eucharist serving as the sign of the New Covenant, making God's family truly <u>universal</u> (<u>katholikos</u> in Greek) otherwise known as the Catholic Church" (34-35). Dr. Hahn does not identify his sixth covenant, and although he contends his ideas are Bible based, it fits *Lumen Gentium*'s altered covenant.

I respectfully submit that the above versions of the Covenant disregard God's commandment of love in interpretation. Instead of nullifying God's New Covenant of forgiveness and His commandment of love, please give us a universal Eucharist as the post-Vatican II New Testament scholars posed to you in 1968.

Concernedly yours,

———————————————

July 15, 2008

Dear Holy Father,

You know best that Jesus' words plainly acknowledged that the New Covenant (see reverse page) was to be ratified and fulfilled in Christ's sacrifice of the Eucharist and the Cross. As God pledged, Jesus performed, and every human being's evil was forgiven forever.

However, my diocesan bishop correctly wrote me that the Catholic Church teaches as dogma that "To receive Holy Communion requires true Catholics [sic] faith and worthiness." God, all knowing, foresaw that men would try to improve on His cleansing and, as indicated by Bishop Wiegand, on His teachings.

God pledged that He alone would imprint the knowledge of Him and His law of love on the least and greatest of us so that we need no church to teach us. However, most everything I know I learned from our Church in God's way.

Since the last days of Jesus Christ, each human person has been immaculately created with immunity to the evil their free wills are naturally expected to do. From the beginning, God deemed this good and forgave our bad conduct by Christ's death.

God's design of redemption included the sacrifice of Calvary and the sacrifice of Eucharist as one piece in thanksgiving. By consuming Jesus Christ's actual flesh, we know God, love God, and serve God as God wishes. But, a removable irritant is the Catholic Church's resistance to Christ's universal Eucharist. It ignores God's law of love and is not True Church so long as it persists with the Church's Eucharist. Please, do something!

Yours in Christ,

_____

July 21, 2008

Dear Holy Father,

Jesus Christ's death ratified and His Last Supper words instituted The New Covenant (Jer 31) to be performed for all humanity (1 Cor 11:25, Mk 14:24, Mt 26:28, Lk 22:20, and reverse page). Thus, we became a new creation, a new generation, and a born again people in the Blood of the Lamb. God performed His pledge to teach us all we need to know about Him and His law of love through Christ's extension of the Covenant from Israelites to redeem all humanity into God's Kingdom. This is done not by any merit on our part, but because God in Goodness loves us and wants to be with us. It is a unilateral covenant due in part with the fact that God husbands us faithfully, but we prove to be constantly unfaithful by nature. So, God saves us and teaches us in our natural state of sinfulness.

However, human beings traditionally change the New Covenant terms. For example, this occurs in the Fourth Gospel, where sinful men translate the terms to a bilateral covenant. We are commanded to believe to be saved, eat to be saved, etc. (John 3:18 or 26:53). Irenaeus may have been biased to add John's inconsistent Gospel as a part of the Canon, but it fit the early Church's traditionalists' translations, such as

Didache 10:6. When Constantine was in control, we agreed to be ruled by a creed and more human regulations. The Church usurped God as teacher and forgiver as it burdened us with its traditions. Its human rules brought us down to where the Church's Eucharist is reserved for only "worthy" Catholics.

Since 2006, my Diocesan Statutes have returned to that trend and established a Church's Eucharist similar to the one Joseph Cardinal Ratzinger championed to be scripturally correct (*God Is Near Us*, p. 60; citing as authority *Didache* 10:6). I assert that Our LORD cringes at my spiritual shepherds' uncharitable Eucharist and arrogance in assuming Church-cleansed souls are purer than those God cleansed. I have been accused of incorrectness in analysis on a basis of Church teaching, an accusation that may be true. Consequently, I welcome any dialogue to clarify that my reasoning and obedience of faith are based on Christ's teachings, to which the Catholic Church has enlightened me since 1960.

What if I am right? If I am right, then my spiritual leaders may be guilty as accessories to the greatest sin in human history. My bishop writes as though he blindly accepts the pre-council teachings as infallibly correct. My Pope does not answer my writings, but his own writings show his deliberate and conscious disregard for the teachings of Vatican II as taught by the New Testament scholars he disputed (p. 59, *Infra*). The Council's *ressourcement* returned us to Christ's Eucharist.

Yours in Christ,

_____

Fred Ithurburn

July 28, 2008

Dear Holy Father,

> "Oh, what a tangled web we weave,
> When first we practice to deceive!"

Walter Scott's words come to mind when I think about your support for the Church's Eucharist after Vatican II. Father Bernard Häring, C.Ss.R. wrote on page 93 of *My Hope for the Church* that two protagonists, Karol Wojtyla and Joseph Ratzinger, moved to accept the Second Vatican Council in principle, though only in modified versions. As leading figures, they persuaded others to their restrictive interpretation.

Clearly, you expressed restrictive scriptural interpretations in rejecting the inclusive Church's Eucharist espoused by our New Testament scholars in 1968/9. As Joseph Cardinal Ratzinger, you edited *God Is Near Us*, and, on pages 59 and 60, you reported your rejection of their open Eucharist idea to reassert the pre-Vatican II traditional Eucharist, which denied most everyone but select Catholics participation in this redemptive Sacrament.

By doing so, it is apparent to me that you latched onto the trailing vestments of Pope John Paul II and pleased other traditionalists entrenched in power at Rome to ride your ambitions into better privileges and positions in the Catholic Church. Your 1968/9 opinion not only assisted you to the papacy, but you, in turn, carried the traditional exclusive Eucharist with you to its present acceptance throughout the Church. You apparently disregarded God's law of love for personal gain, and you nullified God's word in favor of the pre-Vatican II traditions.

Rather than risk another Vatican Council, you later opted for Eucharist Synods wherein bishops selected as loyal to the Pope were under direction of Curial cardinals opposed to subsidiarity. You reduced bishops' collegiality to a verbal fiction. Working Vatican documents to the Synod and later diocesan statutes made sure your opinion on an exclusive Eucharist took effect, so only those of our faith were to receive Holy Communion. My Diocesan Statutes of the Third Diocesan Synod were promulgated in 2006 and were purported to be based on the Bishop's Synod. In truth and fact, they were based on your control of the Synod and pre-Vatican II traditions.

Jesus accurately prophesied in Mark 7:9, "you have made a fine art of setting aside God's commandment in the interests of keeping your traditions!" *Sacramentum Caritatis* belatedly delegated and authorized diocesan bishops' final judgment on these matters, and you thereby misleadingly weaved into your web that the encyclical was based on the Synod of Bishops. Actually, the unlimited centralization over any synodial structure of the Church by your papal government produced the present Eucharist. Thus, it is a product of you alone and, I submit, far removed from the all loving gift to us that Christ so dearly purchased and meant all humanity to experience.

Now that you have attained your goals of privilege and position, what prevents you from ruling for a Eucharist as Christ and God meant for all of humanity to have? Remember, Christ will likely ask you, "After what it costs, why did you appropriate this gift for you and your church alone?" Your taking away of the gift harms so many, and you nullified God's commandment in favor of human tradition for centuries to come. The Catholic Church has become a worshipped god, while Our Lord God is disregarded in your Eucharist. Becoming fully aware of that fact, you also appreciate that you can cure the wrong, and to continue your wrongdoing is willfully and maliciously spiting Christ's mercy.

Yours in Christ,

_____

Dear Holy Father,

You and the traditionalists in the Catholic Church want God to don Jeremiah's rotten loin cloth again. In regard to the Church's Eucharist, you assign Christ's entire work of serving and teaching to an anti-covenantal principle—that God fails to perform adequately. You insist upon the traditional involvement of human precepts to improve upon Christ's cleansing and enlightening of humanity, because you feel that we, the results of God's covenant pledges, are not yet worthy enough to receive Holy Communion without you. Only baptized and reconciled Catholics are worthy of receiving the Eucharist, in your misled opinions.

Can you not see that you thereby deny the unique presence of God in Christ's Eucharist? Your giving of more cleansing power to the Church than to God is an evil principle, an anti-Christ principle, "<u>This is the blasphemy against the Spirit that will not be forgiven,</u> because it negates the evidence of God's saving action in history" (footnote 12, 31 *f* of Matthew).

Later at judgment, you may argue in defense human error or prejudice to Jesus Christ. As an experienced lawyer I advise the better defense, to avoid chastisement or worse, is to now give to all created people the Eucharist that God meant for them to have unconditionally. Rather than chastisements, you will forever receive plaudits.

Concernedly
yours in Christ,

_____

August 27, 2008

Dear Holy Father,

Even though you refuse to respond to my correspondence of concern for the Catholic Church because of its exclusion of many from the Church's Eucharist, I believe from your writings that my concern is warranted. If one was to believe the reasoning of St. Augustine, the Catholic Church is not the Church of Christ. The true Church could not subsist in one that excludes others from its Eucharist. That is what you and your mentor Augustine claimed. You wrote your doctoral dissertation on St. Augustine's argument against the Donatists when he reasoned that, because they lacked *caritas* in excluding members from the sacraments, the true Church could not be found in Donatism (*The New Yorker*, 7/25/05).

In the Second Vatican Council, the top of the hierarchy of the Catholic Church succeeded in paying attention to Jesus' teaching, which included that they not lord over others, but serve the needs of the many. Afterwards, the New Testament scholars confronted you with their criticism of the Church's Eucharist and their contention that Christ meant for all people to be invited to the Lord's Supper. But, you opposed their idea on your less credible interpretation of the Bible, which establishes a Eucharist that excludes most everyone except reconciled Catholics (*God Is Near Us*). Consequently, the Church of Christ subsists in the Catholic Church, but not truly or fully ever since you returned us to the pre-Vatican II's traditional Eucharist, excluding most everyone from the Sacrament.

I am too limited in ability to persuade you to share my concerns about the reality of my spiritual shepherds' negation of God's saving action. Christ's Eucharist was mysteriously meant to include everyone in God's redemptive covenantal benefits. My shepherds, at best, simply analyzed incorrectly, and need obedience of faith to accept the teaching of Christ over traditional teaching of our hierarchies in order to correctly serve us in Christ's way.

Yours from one of
Christ's Catholics,

———————————

September 2, 2008

Dear Holy Father,

Decades ago my pastor Joseph Bishop told me how Pope John XXIII happened to slip through the schemes of the traditionalists and become our pope. Bishop Giovanni Montini was kept in the wings to obtain his red hat, and Pope John was to act in his stead as an interim. The Holy Spirit worked a wonder and gave us the Second Vatican Council with a Shepherd that obeyed Christ rather than the Catholic Church.

Christ gave his life to perform God's covenant and benefit all of humanity. It was an agreement performed by God alone, and we humans benefited from it without any performance on our part. God loves us as we are, and He performed His pledge to totally forgive us through the self-sacrifice of Jesus, fulfilling God's pledges to Jeremiah (Jer 31:33-34). We need no teaching or cleansing, as Christ has perfected us to God's satisfaction. Some may be chastised by Christ later.

Christ's Spirit allowed the Second Vatican Council to renew evidence of God's saving action in history. Christ founded no church, except in the sense of all humans as Christ's Church. So, Pope and bishops found Christ's Church to subsist in the Catholic Church (*Lumen Gentium*). The Glorious Christ's parting words to Peter were to feed his lambs and his sheep, and, in obedience, our New Testament Scholars pressed for a universal Eucharist in 1968 on the basis that Christ intended to exclude no human being from coverage of God's New Covenant (Mk 14:24, and your lecture notes in *Commonweal*, 4/21/06, p. i3). God meant for the Church to feed all His sheep with Christ's Eucharist as an "interdependent" part of God's redemptive action (*God Is Near Us*, p. 29).

However, Christ and Isaiah accurately prophesied about the "hypocrites" in hierarchies who make a fine art of setting aside God's actions to cling to human tradition (Mk 7:1-13). These supposed experts teach mere human precepts as dogma and squeeze out a gnat of a Eucharist that excludes sinners, non-Catholics, and most everyone on earth from Christ's Eucharist. For instance, my diocesan bishop is retiring and leaving statutes promulgated in 2006 that exclude most everyone from our traditionalists' Eucharist, the form the aforesaid New Testament scholars' criticized. Traditionalists may favor the Roman Catholic Church as a world institution, but their nullification of God's Word risks speaking against the Holy Spirit (Mt 12:31 *f*).

Yours from one of
Christ's Catholics,

_____

September 15, 2008

Dear Holy Father,

Bishop William Wiegand announced his wish to retire. I wish him well and am happy to hear this good news. As you know, I copied your letters to him. He also never responded, save for one instance. He wrote a letter to me that plainly established that his mind and heart were closed on the issue of the Church's Eucharist. He wrote that I needed "obedience of faith" to the teaching of the Church, the teaching which had been clear to the Church back to St. Paul, shown in the following, "To receive Holy Communion requires true Catholic faith and worthiness." Earlier, in 2006, he promulgated Diocesan Statutes that ruled out Holy Communion for all non-Christians, most non-Catholics, and some ungraced Catholics, based on your Synod.

Ironically, his motto was "Feed My Lambs." He may never have realized that Christ premised this quoted order upon Peter's affirmation to the question, "do you love me more than these?" To Peter, "these" obviously were his fellow fishermen. In my bishop's case, "these" were his ruling Catholic hierarchy. I tried to write "these" spiritual shepherds that they needed "obedience of faith" to Christ more than to the Church's traditions, but I did so without success. Jesus tried to bluntly tell them the same, (Mk 7:1-13) but "these" minds and hearts closed to cling to centuries of Church tradition.

I also copied my letters to our bishop's replacement Bishop, Jaime Soto. His coat of arms is a promising "Joy and Hope." Hopefully, he loves Christ "more than these" obstructive human teachings that prevent us from freely practicing the Sacrament in Christ's way, as the post-Vatican II scholars contended. Christ plainly told his disciples, "Only one is your teacher, the Messiah" (Mt 23:10). So, Vatican II tried to return us to Christ's way of equal charity to all humans, globally. Its spirit was succeeding until you showed up to return us to a pre-counciliar Church's Eucharist.

Please, for mankind's sake, love Christ "more than these" things that cause you to nullify the redemptive sufferings of Christ. God imprints the fact that He loves us in the minds and hearts of everyone by His own means. On your own biased opinion, you deliberately set aside the mystery of the Eucharist as an interdependent part of Christ's suffering and ongoing redemption of all humans. Christ teaches us that all are to take Holy Communion. We obey simply because Christ says so, and, in some mysterious way, we are thereby imprinted or transformed with God's covenantal gifts of knowledge and renewal.

Yours for any discussion,

_____

September 26, 2008

Dear Holy Father,

Your Holiness and your hierarchy practice a policy of lording over us lay Catholics. I evidence this by your disrespecting of my letters of concern for the Church's Eucharist. Our Dogmatic Constitution on the Church (*Lumen Gentium*) obligates me to express my concerns, but it also vests me with the duties of my spiritual shepherds to "recognize and promote the dignity" of my concerns for the good of the Church (Ch. IV, "The Laity," No. 37). My expressed concern, however, is that any excommunication negates God's saving means in the Eucharist. Because all my shepherds ignore me, I try to refer the controversy in contention to all the people of God, the Church of Christ, in keeping with Christ's teachings (Mt 18:17). It allows people self-appraisals.

As a means to reach the people, I am contemplating a lawsuit against the Roman Catholic Diocese of Sacramento for its willful withholding of the Eucharist. I may include, for all those deprived of their divine rights to the Bread of Life, a class action based on willful acts of occasioning personal injury to them in violation of §1714 of the California Civil Code. I additionally aim to bring to the attention of the Church of Christ, made up of everyone in the world, the concerns that I expressed in all my letters to you and to my diocesan bishop, which you both chose to ignore.

Archbishop George Niederauer of San Francisco recently told us that the practice of the Church "is to accept the conscientious self-appraisal of each person" who approaches for Communion, (*The Catholic Herald* 9/6/08). I am open to discussions for settling the controversy as I am reluctant to sue my Church. I await hearing from the Diocese, because you stated in *Sacramentum Caritatis*, "final judgment on these matters belong to the diocesan bishop." I would compromise for an open Communion without any limitation except the "conscientious self-appraisal of each person."

I await recognition of my concern,

September 26, 2008

Most Revs. William Wiegand & Jaime Soto
Catholic Diocese of Sacramento
2110 Broadway
Sacramento, CA 95819-2608

Dear Bishop Wiegand and Bishop Soto,

On the reverse page, I have again copied the letter to Pope Benedict XVI on the subject of filing a lawsuit for the §1714 Civil Code personal injuries that your Diocesan Statutes have inflicted on most of God's people living in the Diocese of Sacramento. I hereby want to establish that it is not an idle threat. Perhaps you should advise your attorneys and liability insurance carriers of my letters threatening litigation. Better yet, talk with me.

It has been my practice to telegraph my punches when I intend to sue, so that negotiations might be able to forego formal court actions. They may argue that there is no precedence for such causes of action, but this case may establish the remedy for an obvious wrong that Vatican II revealed that traditional Catholics have been committing for centuries. Pope Benedict, as Joseph Cardinal Ratzinger, wrote of these contentions by our New Testament scholars' 1968 criticisms of the Church's Eucharist and their claims that Christ's intent was to have an open invitation for sinners and non-Catholics to His Eucharist (*God Is Near Us*, p. 59). God's saving action is being nullified. For every wrong, we should have a remedy.

I may have tried more tort cases to verdict than any other attorney throughout Northern California. Should I be pressed to argue damages, I suggest that what you deprive people of receiving belongs to everyone. The Eucharist is the most valuable pearl of Catholics. Non-Catholics who will set as jurors in judgment could assess reasonable monetary sums for each member of a class suit, and thus be able to award a substantial sum of compensatory damages.

Before we face such problems, I am open to alternative suggestions from spiritual shepherds who *Lumen Gentium* represented and who would hopefully advise us. Through "dialogue between the laity and their spiritual leaders," we can reach allowances that the whole Church should make, allowances that "may more effectively fulfill its mission for the life of the world" (Ch. IV, No. 37).

Bishop Thomas Gumbleton suggests, "Don't excommunicate. Communicate" (*NCR*, 9/19/08). Please respond.

Fred B. Ithurburn

cc: His Holiness Pope Benedict XVI,
        Rev. Blaise Berg

October 1, 2008

Dear Holy Father,

My Diocesan Bishop William Keith Wiegand was installed as my spiritual shepherd in January, 1994. He replaced Bishop Francis Anthony Quinn after strident outcries from "traditionalists" complaining about Quinn's Vatican II ecumenical outreach. Bishop Wiegand informed us that his style was different and that he runs a tight ship. He admitted that his task was to ensure compliance with the Church's teachings and exact obedience to Holy See guidelines. Such a guideline was your recently issued *Catechism of the Catholic Church*, with Father Joseph Corapi appointed to preach it. As one of the latter's students, I recall Corapi stated that the Catechism was as credible as the Bible, and Tradition was capitalized because of its elevated authority. His opinions, those mentioned and others, polarized priests and left me bewildered on where the Church of Christ now subsists.

In a later telling history of the diocese, among Bishop Wiegand's proud moments was his 2003 public urge to our Governor Gray Davis that with his pro-choice stand he should choose to abstain from receiving Holy Communion. He meant to teach Davis, a Catholic, not to excommunicate him. However, Bishop Raymond Burke of Wisconsin decided on excommunicating pro-choice Democrats, and cited Bishop Wiegand as his inspiration. In telling the history of the Diocese we, of course, read of Burke's inspiration as if it is ours to brag about.

In his August 4, 2007 letter to me, Bishop Wiegand plainly stated his idea of Church's teachings, in part, as follows, "The teaching of the Church is very clear since the time at least of St. Paul. To receive Holy Communion requires true Catholics faith and worthiness." Thus, his Diocese Statutes of the Third Diocesan Synod conform exactly to restrictions of the traditional Church's Eucharist, the Catechism—the working documents sent by the Vatican to the bishops in Synod, the teachings of the Church as Bishop Wiegand understands them. Christ's last words are absent from these teachings, and his love is squeezed to gnat size in the statutes that Wiegand promulgated.

Obviously, the teachings of Jesus Christ in his institution of the Eucharist and the ratification of the New Covenant (Jer 31:33) by his death can never successfully imprint incentive to open our Eucharist to sinners and non-Catholics in the closed mind and heart of Bishop Wiegand. Hopefully, his successor will follow Jesus and not misleading Catholic Tradition and Traditionalists. But, as Vicar of Christ, you must repent and assure that God's saving action in Eucharist continues to be as redemptive as Christ and not as Wiegand intended, or else answer to Christ why his sheep are not fed.

———————————

October 6, 2008

Dear Holy Father,

On the reverse page is a copy of an article my daughter-in-law wrote for a local paper. The story is about my grandson Peter. Peter and his two sisters have yet to be baptized, but they are God's people and members of the human race who are baptized in the Blood of the Covenant. Christ has these least born into the kingdom of God to be greater than John the Baptizer (Mt 11:11). But, not one of them is worthy to receive the Church's Eucharist, according to you and my bishops.

God's Gift to You

You lectured in 1968/69 that Christ's Gospel "for many" (Mk 14:24) prevents the church from becoming a select community of the righteous, a community that condemns the wayward masses to perdition (*Commonweal*, p. 13, 4/21/08). My unbaptized grandchildren, however, are members of the wayward masses you defined, and the Dioceses of Sacramento has expressly excluded them, along with all non-Christians, from Christ's interdependent extension in God's saving action by means of the Church's Eucharist. This is your Eucharist, not Christ's.

You reject the Gospel of Christ's words at the Last Supper to rationalize scriptural hearsay, such as Jn 13:10, 1 Cor 11:27 *ff*, and *Didache* 10:6 to justify your Eucharist (*God Is Near Us*, p. 60). Those Christ redeemed to be born as his siblings, including those mentioned above, have God given rights to share the Eucharist that you uncharitably withhold from them. By forsaking the Lord's Gospel of love and Christ's universal Communion of God's saving action in history, you make Catholicism a salvation for the select few, thus making it a non-Christian community. Kerry Kennedy's *Being Catholic Now* states it is instead about loving, truth, and "building a community where we love one another" (*Catholic Herald*, 10/4/08). You negate God's saving action in Christ to cling to traditions of the Church Eucharist to earn you a "Woe!"

Thus, my daughter-in-law and her children are among the least to greatest whom God adequately assures know Him, according to the New Covenant. You need no teacher but Christ alone to overcome any "obedience of faith" to traditions that blind my bishop. You do not have his defense of ignorance or obedience to Church infallibility. So, repent! Please.

Sincerely,

Divine Intervention
by Hope Ithurburn

It was an experience I never asked for, but will cherish forever.

I was in labor, ready to give birth to our third child, a son, via cesarean section. My doctor chose to delay the delivery since the Labor and Delivery unit had only one surgery room available. It worried me to know that there were surgeries scheduled back-to-back throughout the day, and I was not one of them. I tried to stay positive and reassured myself that we would be okay; we were in the hospital and if anything went wrong, we'd be in safe hands.

A few hours into labor, I had unknowingly suffered a uterine rupture. It was at that point that the internal bleeding began. Simultaneously, another expectant mother to the right of me started to experience complications and began hemorrhaging. My selfish thoughts of my baby and my welfare were now redirected towards the mother and unborn child just feet away from me.

After a flurry of "violent" contractions, which accompany uterine ruptures, a flood of emotions overwhelmed me. I began crying, sobbing, praying, swearing and was desperate for help. There was no indication that our baby was in danger until the monitor tracking his heart rate alerted us to the sudden drop. Due to the uterine rupture, the placenta had separated from my uterine wall causing the baby's head to tear through the protective sac.

Unbeknown to us, God was already working in the surgery room, awaiting our arrival. There, a woman was seconds away from receiving her epidural prior to her scheduled c-section. The anesthesiologist was interrupted by a call on the "emergency" phone. He was told to stop everything and that a patient needing an emergency c-section was on her way in. The nurses were planning to rush in the woman next to me. Luckily, they were able to stabilize her condition; and now, the one headed to the surgery room was me.

Upon entering, it was eerie seeing the surgeons, sterilized medical instruments and team of pediatric doctors lined up -- meant for someone else, but given to us. Just as the nurse was putting the mask over my mouth, I paused and prayed to God. I asked him to save my baby, I told him that I loved him and that I trusted him enough to let go. At that moment, I was totally overcome with peace. It was only then that I was able to entirely submit to God. I then prayed, "Do your will, whatever that may be". Two hours later, I woke up in the recovery room with my husband at my side.

Over the next few hours, I was still in shock. I struggled to make sense of what happened, why it happened and what went so wrong. I attempted to verbalize my gratitude to God by repeating my most sincere, heart-felt "thank you's" over and over again.

(cont. on pg. 11 - DIVINE)

DIVINE
cont. from pg. 4

It has been over a year now and I replay every detail of our story in my head almost every day. Our precious baby, Peter, came into the world not breathing, completely unprotected and at risk of suffering permanent neurological damage. He is now one year old and a strong, vibrant, busy little boy. I continue to be in awe of God's power and mercy that was poured over us that day. He has honored me by allowing me to capture just a small glimmer of his majesty.

God is here among us, God is working when we think he is not and God holds the power to do the unimaginable. ∎

October 13, 2008

Dear Holy Father,

At Mass, I hopefully pray in our Eucharistic Prayer, "Lord, remember your Church throughout the world, make us grow in love together with Benedict XVI, our Pope, William Wiegand, our bishop . . . ." Vatican II established "your Church" to be the Church of Christ, which subsists in the Catholic Church (*Lumen Gentium*). The congregation, my pope, and my bishops, however, consider "your Church" to be identified with the Catholic Church. And the lack of perceived movement in their love becomes more obvious as we distance ourselves from Vatican II. I think you and your predecessor's doing is the Magisterium. Your tradition persuaded my diocesan bishop to your restrictive interpretation of Vatican II and to reject the post Vatican II New Testament scholars' contention for a universal Eucharist.

My spiritual leaders do not agree on their respective rationale to support the Church's Eucharist. My Bishop reasons on basis of millenniums of Church tradition. Instead, you argued on the ambiguous hearsay of John, Paul, and *Didache* (*God Is Near Us*, p. 60). You both refuse ressourcement to Jesus' plain words at the Last Supper, "take this all of you," and you both refuse ressourcement to His reference to the New Covenant, which he instituted interdependent with the Eucharist. At Mass last week, St. Paul called Galatians "stupid" for not following Christ's teachings in favor of listening to others. You two tragically follow these others' opinions to deny most people Christ's Eucharist. The failure to reach you of Christ and my concerns is frustrating.

However, a thoughtful comfort has come to me. It seems that Christ's New Covenant assures me that no matter what wrongdoing either of you do; God's love will make it good. Still, there will be fewer people thanking God for goodness by means of the Eucharist than the many Christ intended. Christ may not accept this as does God, but hereafter he can mercifully seek justice and chastisement for you negating his gifts of gratitude from the Eucharist of the many, who were never invited to the thanksgiving banquet by either of you.

Yours in Christ,

_____

October 20, 2008

Dear Holy Father,

You are aware that *Lumen Gentium* (see reverse page's example) markedly changed the terms contained in the New Covenant text of Jeremiah 31:34, which Christ ratified and instituted as the New Testament. For instance, the dotted space on through the end of their purported quote on the reverse page should read:

> 34. And they shall teach no more every man his neighbor, and every man his brother, saying: Know the Lord, for all shall know me from the least of them even to the greatest, says the Lord: for I will forgive their iniquity and I will remember their sin no more.

However, changing the contents of the agreement frees the Church to continue making loose declarations that the distorted Covenant allows, such as "this" covenant that Christ instituted in his Blood that calls together those who believe in Him as the new People of God. No longer does Christ extend the Covenant (Jer 31:33-34) from Israel to redeem the world, which would keep with God's pledge to forgive and forget his people's evil. Now, the scribes select only the few who believed in Christ to be God's People. God seemingly did not remove our reproaches and inability to know Him (Is 25:7-8).

Also, by deleting the provision that God alone is our teacher, we returned the Church to teaching mere human precepts, which lack *caritas,* as dogma. Among dogmatic Church teaching is a Church's

Eucharist which excludes most people and denies us the grace and freedom to love our neighbors indiscriminately. God resigns to our sinning ways, says we are "good," and pardons our ways as okay by forgiving and forgetting our evil in the blood of Christ. However, we know that the okay conduct of the 1960's disturbed the common sense of God's imprinted law in us. Christ's grace demonstrated that we should act for the common good, and his Eucharist memorialized how to love and strengthen us to proclaim love to the world.

Since you never made your opinion on an exclusive Eucharist (*God Is Near Us*, p. 60) into dogma, and instead passed the buck to diocesan bishops in *Sacramentum Caritatis* (1908), I suspect that you fear confronting Christ or the Curia. I pray that you obey Christ's law of love. That is to say, give us Christ's universal Eucharist, which complies with fulfillment of the true Covenant that makes all of us destined through Christ (Eph 1:3-10). For by love, by Christ's grace, are we saved, but not because of works such as believing in Christ (Eph 2:1-10).

Yours in Christ,

_____

October 24, 2008

Dear Holy Father,

Writing this monologue to my disregarding spiritual shepherds seems to be my Cross to bear. If the Spirit of God does not bring some good out of this effort, then its imitation of Christ escapes me. I feel somewhat like Sisyphus rolling this rock uphill, but instead of it rolling back as I near the top of the hill, each time I write I find I am in a trench and have made no progress, whatsoever. Where is this fatherly love (*Lumen Gentium*, Ch. IV, No. 37) I was supposed to receive for my efforts?

In his day, St. Paul's writings were well received, but from the time he was knocked off his ass, his mind was imprinted with the good news of God's plan of salvation. He wrote that before the world began, God chose us, in Christ, to be blameless in His sight and to be full of love. Note that this is consistent with God's New Covenant pledges, fulfilled in the Blood of Christ, to forgive and forget our evildoing and to imprint in us knowledge of God and His law to love each other. Paul wrote that we were likewise destined as adopted children, through Christ Jesus, to do the will of God here and hereafter in praising Jesus Christ (Eph 1:3-10). I submit that the Eucharist serves this earthly purpose of praising, thanking, and that all might gloriously adore Jesus Christ at Communion (Eph 2:3-10). Paul also wrote that faith to move mountains was nothing if it lacked love (1 Cor 13:2). He cautioned those who unlovingly discriminate against the body by failing to recognize the whole human race in Eucharist, thus bringing judgment upon themselves (1 Cor 11:29). The chastisement is greater for the servants who know better. Paul repeated, "This is not our doing, it is God's gift" of Christ that salvation is ours (Eph 2:8). Please inform the Catholic Church of these truths, since what you say is well-received by Catholics.

Yet, the Church's Eucharist, which you dare to champion, excommunicates those many saved by God, those who have not voluntarily entered into the mystery of Jesus Christ (*God Is Near Us*, p. 60). *Lumen Gentium* (Ch. 11, No. 9) excludes those God saved by the Blood of the New Covenant (Jer 31:31-34)—the "many" who do not also "believe in Christ"—from the People of God. Understandably, *Lumen Gentium* is devious in its distortion of the New Covenant when it deletes God's pledges and disenfranchises "many" of God's people. I contend that God's law of love (Mk 7:1-13) makes up for our failings, instead of our works of will, belief, and faith, as God already has perfected us. You know better than to permit this blasphemy, as evidenced by what you lectured, preached, and published before your promotions up through the hierarchy. You previously asserted, in effect, that to deny anyone the Church or the Eucharist prevents the Catholic Church from being true Church, or it prevents the Church of Christ from subsisting in the Catholic Church because it simply offends God's law of love. I argue that it nullifies God's revelation of Christ's saving action in history and is anti-Christ.

Yours in Christ,

October 27, 2008

Dear Holy Father,

Lumen Gentium obliged me to express my opinions concerning the good of the Church's Eucharist, and my spiritual leaders were to consider them with fatherly love, test them, and hold fast to that which is good (*cf* 1 Thes 5:19, No. 13 and No. 37). By reason of my efforts, I have come to know of another concern which I am also obligated to express for the good of the Church. It is the distortion in Chapter II of *Lumen Gentium* and its deliberate misstating of the New Covenant (Jer 31:31-34). I trust that this concern will earn more response than did my opinions concerning the Church's Eucharist, because I read it as clearer evidence of an anti-Christ blasphemy by my spiritual leaders in the Catholic Church.

In my previous letters, I spelled out how the authors of *Lumen Gentium* deleted essential portions of God's pledges in the New Covenant, and I explained how this negates God's evidence of performing the forgiveness of all human evildoing through Christ. The authors also confuse Christ's unveiling in everyone the knowledge of God as Love in law and Being. The scribes of Church law thereby blaspheme the Holy Spirit by negating God's unilateral action to save humanity from death, and their defining of only those who successfully believe in Christ to be the messianic people is anti-Christ. Their teaching is based on the lie that Christ needs teachers to teach us to believe as they do, and we thusly require the Catholic Church teachings to know God.

However, I think that you, Pope Benedict XVI, were called to remedy this uncharitable wrongdoing in *Lumen Gentium*, as well as the Church's Eucharist. Your earlier lectures at Tübingen show you were aware of the need to change the Catholic Church for the good of the Church of Christ. You taught that Jesus did not intend to found a church. The one that evolved, you felt, had been founded not in Jesus authorizing Peter (Mt 16:18), but was instituted with the Eucharist and his Last Supper words. You noted your opinions of how instituting the Eucharist and launching His redemption were interdependent, as Jesus linked his sacrifice "for many" (Is 53 and Mk 14:24) with the new covenant in his blood (Jer 31). You lectured that the "for many" prevents the Church from selecting less than the whole human race for saving by Christ's Blood. God's love would not have created any individual to be left out for condemnation (*Commonweal*, 4/21/06). But that is the very discrimination that the Catholic Church now constitutionally endorses. In your doctoral dissertation, you wrote that if we regard God's commandment of love as ruling, then the true Church cannot be founded on the exclusion of anyone. To redeem the world, rather than cling to dogma of Church bias wherein Catholics are selected worthier and holier than others, we must accept that Christ has redeemed the world in the Blood of the New Covenant. God does it all, not us. He made all men equal and pure in Christ's death. Thus, the Church of Christ subsists in the Catholic Church, but not so long as the Church's Eucharist and Constitution uncharitably exclude others.

Sincerely,

November 3, 2008

Dear Holy Father,

My diocesan bishop, Bishop William Wiegand, retired this month. He once wrote to me on the subject of the Church's Eucharist to tell me that my analysis was incorrect and that I needed "obedience of faith" to accept the teaching of the Church. He added that the "teaching of the Church is very clear" that "to receive Holy Communion requires true Catholics faith and worthiness." That response, in effect, is the extent of fatherly advice that I received and expect to receive from the spiritual shepherds that the Catholic Church has furnished me "through the organs erected by the Church for this purpose" (No. 37, *Lumen Gentium*, Ch. IV, "The Laity").

Bishop Jaime Soto replaces Bishop Wiegand, and though he has been addressed on copies of my letters to you, I have no idea what he thinks on the subject. By copy of this specific letter, I invite him to discuss both the subject of the Church's Eucharist and the additional concern I have for the Catholic Church and its Dogmatic Constitution on the Church (*Lumen Gentium*). Since our Diocesan Statutes from 2006 were likely authorized by your *Sacramentum Caritatis* of 4/2/07, he should be targeted with our communications.

In a nutshell, I contend that Vatican II's Pope John XXIII and our worldwide bishops together espoused a global church and an inclusive Eucharist based on the New and Everlasting Covenant—God forgave every human being of sins through Christ's blood at conception. At conception, in even the least of us, God imprinted how to know Him so as to prevent such teachings as prejudiced Bishop Wiegand's, in order to promulgate our Diocesan Statutes. Like Jesus, we increase in wisdom with experience of God and man (Lk 2:52; Mk 6:38, 8:27; and Phil 217).

I more recently added a supplemented caution that I suspect the Catholic Church, by distorting the New Covenant (Jer 31:33) in Ch. II, No. 9, of *Lumen Gentium*, is guilty of negating God's evidence for Christ in our salvation. We now find a church based on our belief or faith, rather than the commandment of love that He desires. I assert that the likes of Constantine, his creed, and his martialized church still influence us as it did Bishop Wiegand in his obedience to the Church's teaching instead of Christ's teachings.

Sincerely,

———————————————

Dear Holy Father,

People of the light do not do as people prudently do in the world. As Jesus demonstrated in his passion, the reason they don't is their love of others at least as well as they love themselves (Lk 16 "The Wily Manager"). The prudent steward has nothing on the people in Rome who manage the Catholic Church, and Jesus could have used them as a standard of world prudence.

For example, take the Church's Eucharist—*Lumen Gentium*'s distortion of the New Covenant (Jer 31). Clinging to Church tradition, only graced Catholics are deemed worthy to receive Holy Communion. Deleting terms of Christ's testament (Jer 31:34: "No longer will they have need to teach their friends and kinsmen how to know the Lord . . . for I will forgive their evildoing and remember their sin no more") limits those redeemed by Christ to "those who believe in Christ" (*Lumen Gentium* Ch. II "on the People of God," No. 9).

Jesus progressively learned through his life that he was the messiah and to be used by God as the instrument for the redemption of all people created by God. By the Blood of God's covenant, everyone's sins are forgiven and forgotten. By the same last will and testament of Christ, the teachings of how to know the Lord will be done by Jesus Christ, imprinting love as a law in each of us, even infants, to the extent that God desires. He never expected to be usurped by a "messianic people."

The Church of Christ evolved from the institution of Christ's words at the Last Supper, and its purpose was not forgiving or teaching in addition to what Christ furnished by his life and death. It was to be a means to tell the story of Jesus and serve His actual presence, mainly in a memorial thanksgiving meal to which everyone redeemed was invited to be transformed by Christ Himself. All would be transformed to love God and each other as Jesus showed us.

Where have we in the Catholic Church parted from the ideals of Pope John XXIII and the bishops in council, who were in Spirit correcting us in *ressourcement*? The bishops in Synod today might appreciate your enlightened thoughts.

Yours in Christ,

_____

November 10, 2008

Dear Holy Father,

The truth about China's period under Maoism bursts forth from the likes of Jung Chang and her book *Wild Swan*. She lived the life as you experienced under Adolph Hitler's reign. Mao Zedong made himself a god to secure greater control of his communists. The people ceased thinking and they surrendered their thoughts to Mao's cult. Intolerance to protest became ingrained in the people, and Mao turned them into his ultimate weapon to divide and conquer any who might dare question him.

You experienced a similar dictatorship in your youth in Germany. Your familiarity with such rulers makes you more appreciative of why Jesus stated that the spiritual leaders of his Church would not lord it over other members—because power has its own corruptive force. Yet, we find that to be the situation, since Pope John XXIII, as our higher hierarchy in the Church, artfully set aside God's law of love for traditions of an exclusive Eucharist. We Catholics obsequiously followed you rulers because we want to believe.

Christ died to redeem the world, and He thereby fulfilled God's New and Everlasting Covenant (Jer 31). His testament was to be executed without our assistance. As God pledged, Christ's blood pardons every conceived human of evildoing. Whatever residual remains at death, Jesus Christ will judge and chastise us to make us worthy of our inheritance, together. God does it all as a gift. In fact, God mandated no need for teachings other than Christ's. So, however Jesus' testament is probated, God wills that we all are saved no matter what we do, good or evil. The peace heralded at Christmas was for freedom with salvation upon Christ's death. We inherit this New Testament regardless of the Catholic Church's misrecognition of the body of Christ to be less than all humanity.

I suspect you know this, and you know how to know God as Love, who will not waste any one created. Because God imprints in us how to know Him, we learn by naturally living these self-evident truths of Love. The Catholic Church will come to obey God's commandment of love in time, as did the people of anti-Christ worldly rulers, once it quits teaching and ruling an anti-Christ Catholicism. Now, you are best situated to follow Christ and bring Catholics and the world to love just as Christ demonstrated in his last hours. You must learn and teach the self-evident truth that all men are created equal in the context of the Eucharist by, through, and in Christ, so that Christ can better do his thing.

Yours in love,

November 12, 2008

Dear Holy Father,

A book authored by Father Gordon Douglas of Seattle, titled *"Hey, Father!"* prompts this letter. It effects how I write to you. At the beginning of my thoughts, the Catholic Church's Eucharist was so obviously un-Christian that, as an issue to be controverted, I hoped it would last until I was the one who received credit for pointing out the antichristian qualities. But on reading Father Douglas' book, I will temper down my ardor for advocacy and accept that the Spirit of God may have someone else in mind to cure the wrong. I certainly have made no progress for all my efforts.

Although not a Passionist Father, Father Douglas argues that the Cross is the identifiable sign to the world of the love story between God and each one of us. It speaks of our rifts with God and His constant reconciliation efforts with us. God's patience is often tested, "For they broke my covenant and I grew weary of them, says the Lord . . . ." But then, in Christ, God Himself performed the entire new covenant to save all of us, without relying on any contribution by our goodness, whatsoever.

In fact and truth, Christ apparently provided the Eucharist to spread the story of the Cross and allow everyone a chance to appreciate God's love and love Our Lord in turn. But since Vatican II and centuries before, a "dog-in-the-manger" attitude of the Catholic hierarchy has squeezed out gnats of human dogmas to cling to Church tradition and disregard God's commandment of impartially loving others as Vatican II *ressourcement* corrected us to do.

Father Douglas obeys the old traditional Catholicism, but he retains an open heart. He admits to avoiding "For Life" gatherings because of the lack of love expressed by the self-righteous. His faith in the Church's teachings is good enough for him, and so it was with myself for years before my discerning skepticism troubled me to focus my faith in crucified Christ. I write to you in this developed vein because I think that you too should be burdened with the conflict between Christ's teachings and the Catholic Church's teachings. Your obedience to the latter causes exclusion of many from our select company. However, you stand able to cure our less-than-all-loving Church. Your inconsistent past writings and preaching offer me hope for recovery of Catholicism to be truly catholic, not caught in codependent behavior towards erroneous authority. You should simply correct Catholics into compassionately reaching out to all left out of our Church and our Eucharist. The Catholic Church handles Christ's last will as though he died intestate. But, he willed God's love to benefit all humanity, every individual one of us, and you can enforce Christ's will by distributing Christ's body and blood in Eucharist to everyone on earth as heirs apparent.

Yours in love,

Fred Ithurburn

November 14, 2008

Dear Holy Father,

We people often proclaim the mystery of faith that "when we eat this bread and drink this cup, we proclaim your death, Lord Jesus, until you come in glory." We obediently do this, but not in company with "the many" (Mk 14:24), whom Jesus ordered us to share him with in his parting words. Your transcribed lecture notes of 1968/9 acknowledged "the many" to include every created body (*Commonweal,* 4/21/08). However, you now disclaim non-Catholics and others from "the many," and they equally need nourishment to proclaim Christ crucified. You thusly show willingness to condemn many to perdition because they are not the select few favored by *Lumen Gentium* or the Church's Eucharist.

Anti-Christs are those of us who translate the words of Christ "Take this, all of you . . ." to negate God's saving action in Eucharist for all our excommunicated siblings in Christ. You wrote your doctoral dissertation on St. Augustine with concluding that Donatism was not true Church because of its exclusion of priests from its sacraments. True Church cannot exist if it lacks Christ's fundamental virtue of love. It is self-evident that we all are created equal, are equally cleansed, and are to be impartially fed in Holy Communion. The anti-Christs, who disregard God's saving action to love each other as Christ demonstrated, may also bring judgment on themselves (1 *Cor* 11:29). I hope to hear their explanations to Jesus Christ, explanations denied to me now, of why they dared deny anyone Holy Communion.

I do not know if anyone reads these messages. But if so, why are you, the reader, not doing something about this plain blasphemy against the Spirit of Jesus Christ (*The New American Bible*, footnote Mt 12. 31 *f*)? You who deliberately do nothing actually negate the evidence of God's saving action in history, while you who neglect to act may be accessories to the anti-Christ attempts that cause the body of Christ to be uncharitably limited only to Catholics. Obviously, my futile efforts need your help, or the help of someone who loves Christ or humanity as a whole more than he loves the Catholic Church.

Yours open to discussion,

November 17, 2008

Dear Holy Father,

You recently hosted a three-day Catholic-Muslim forum where you naively told Muslim clergy and scholars that we must overcome our misunderstandings. In 2006, you angered Muslims by correctly pointing out Islam's links to violence and suggesting that they must be more reasonable in interpreting their faith. My futile tries to dialogue with you prove that reason is not our common language, but love may be. You might share Eucharist with Islam and let Love work.

I think that we experience the closed minds and hearts of people having "obedience to faith" in the teaching of their respective churches. It is the same problem I have in creating a dialogue on the Eucharist with the spiritual leaders of my Church. There exists no Christian reason for you to refuse to think and discuss the concerns I wrote to you for years. Islam might regard Christ as an agent of God's love, but you miss occasions to invite Muslims to Eucharist and thus allow God's agency to act. By the same reasoning, the refusal to consider my letters with fatherly love, as *Lumen Gentium* suggests, closes your mind and heart to being informed of the obvious.

Had Christians obeyed the teachings of Christ from his last living hours two thousand years ago, Muslims would be free to worship with non-Muslims, and vice-versa, anywhere in the world today. Mohammed may not have felt the need of a religion or a book. Some of us do not believe in Christ as Lord, but many accept Jesus as God's agent of love. Christ believed his mission included ratifying God's New Covenant (Jer 31), and He excruciatingly instituted it as His testamentary disposition to all humans. Thus, God's pledges of forgiving and teaching were freely pledged to every human heir. We need no Catholic Church, no Bible, no Islam, no Qu'ran, etc. to state a less charitable testament of Christ when we have a testament that includes a universal inheritance bequeathed to everybody. But the Catholic Church fails to obey

Christ's order of salvation, and it fails even to feed all his sheepfolds the Eucharist that he fatally suffered to furnish in order to share with them in love.

Reasoning, understanding, and beliefs are nothing if we do not love each other as Christ taught. Let Christ do His thing now by sharing Eucharist with Muslims and everyone else. For millenniums, all our efforts to reason resulted in anti-Christ divisions throughout the world and within Catholicism itself. As our spiritual leader, you should appreciate the problem, but for some reason that escapes me, you refuse to perform in Christ's way—toward a universal Eucharist and Church. I wonder if you possibly fear an Inquisition of those in power, or if you merely fear the failure to justify their choice in you to champion their *cosa nostra* and secure their offices.

Yours in love,

_____

November 19, 2008

Dear Holy Father,

As a parting gift to my diocesan bishop the Most Reverend William Wiegand, let me share Jesus' words and actions at his own parting. As the paschal lamb (Ex 12) and the suffering servant who sacrifices himself "for many" (Is 53), Jesus voluntarily endured an excruciating death "for many" (Mk 14) to fulfill God's pledges in the New Covenant (Jer 31). These are the teachings of Professor Joseph Ratzinger, according to his typescript lectures of 1968/9. Jesus' Last Supper words were interdependent with his sacrifices on Calvary and at Mass.

I hereby spell out my analysis of the thinking of Jesus, as translated from the Synoptics, which Bishop Wiegand wrote was "simply incorrect" in analysis (see reverse page, letter 8/4/07). Let me simplify a syllogism:

1) An expressed purpose for Jesus willing to die was to fulfill the benefits God pledged in the New Covenant for the benefit of His people—all people God created;

2) God pledged to forgive their evildoing and they all, even to the least, shall know how to know the Lord, a pledge Christ fulfilled by fatally bleeding in order to fulfill God's will and redeem us all to be One.

Consequently, the phrase "for many" means everyone, and no one human, no church, and no Tradition negates the evidence in history of God's saving action without blaspheming against the Spirit (Mt 12, 31 *f*). So, the blood of the Lamb frees of sin every prostitute practicing her/his occupation, every recidivist imprisoned and practicing his vice, and every clergyman who clings to tradition and denies God's commandment to love and include everyone in Eucharist, and they may see the great light in their darkness. In his trial of chastisement, Jesus Christ still has judgment, leaving us at peace to his mercy.

On creating us, God knew we were sinners, and as such, God deemed us to be good. In us, God imprinted how to know Him, and by gracing us with the demonstration of love by Jesus Christ in his Cross and his Eucharist, He teaches us love of God and love of each other in the world.

Truthfully, I do not state the above in "obedience of faith" to Church teaching. But, it analyzes what I, perhaps the least of us, believe is likely the teaching of God, in Jesus Christ. It certainly is not the teaching of the Church or anyone else who the Covenant mandates against teaching us contra Christ.

Bon Voyage to Bishop Wiegand,

DIOCESE OF SACRAMENTO

2110 Broadway • Sacramento, California 95818 • 916, 733-0200 • Fax 916, 733-0215

OFFICE OF THE BISHOP

August 4, 2007

Mr. Fred B. Ithurburn
506 Second Street
Yuba City, CA 95991

Dear Fred:

I write to acknowledge receipt of your letter of August 1, 2007.

The teaching of the Church is very clear since the time at least of St. Paul. To receive Holy Communion requires true Catholics faith and worthiness. You are simply incorrect in your analysis and need the "obedience of faith" to accept the teaching of the Church.

A good theologian you might discuss this with – and also well-known to you – is Father Blaise Berg.

Be assured of my prayers and best wishes.

Sincerely in Christ,

WILLIAM K. WEIGAND
Bishop of Sacramento

cc: Fr. Blaise Berg

o

November 21, 2008

Dear Holy Father,

Fox's Book of Martyrs mentions an Englishman in Rome who attacks a bishop in procession. From the bishop, the young man snatches the Host and tramples it on the ground stating, "Ye wretched idolaters, who neglect the true God, to adore a morsel of bread." Under torture he claims, "It was the will of God that I should do as I did." Pope Pius the Fourth (A.D. 1560) sentences him to have his right hand cut off and later burnt to death, which gains the man a Protestant's martyrdom.

The violence of Islam's history that you criticized in 2006 gained martyrdom for nineteen Muslims, whose actions resulted in our 9/11 World Trade Center destruction. Violence with martyrs appears in our Church's history of Crusades and Inquisitions. Also, the discrimination practiced today in our Church's exclusive Eucharist and *Dogmatic Constitution* (*Lumen Gentium*), which favors graced Catholics, condemns most everyone else to hell. The silence, which you impose on me when my shepherds in Christ uncharitably disdain responding to my letters' concerns, oppresses closer to home. These are forms of our Church's uncharitable violence and oppression. Your refusal to respond to me violates *Lumen Gentium*'s provision that you consider my concerns "with fatherly love" (Ch. IV, No. 37), a breach of law endowed on me by our Dogmatic Constitution on the Church.

Let us consider how differently our non-violent Jesus Christ accepted his crucifixion, an event far uglier than being trampled. He lovingly prayed that God forgive those harming him. Jesus willingly and expressly died for all, to have God forgive our evildoing and remember our sins no more. The Catholic Church selfishly erases this term of Christ's last will and denies all but Catholics what Jesus purchased so dearly. The Church's conduct to enhance itself loses Christ's love lesson on how to know God and God's law of love. Christ alone is the key to how to know the Lord and His law as Love. To his teaching, Christ expressly added the Eucharist meal to remember him and to nourish us with "the blood of the new and everlasting covenant . . . shed for all so that sins may be forgiven" (*Eucharistic Prayer*). Let his key open your mind to do what Christ does.

Later, Jesus Christ will also judge us mercifully and give a hearing to some who merit chastisement. You holier ones may explain why so many of us are excluded from the Lord's Supper and inheriting His Last Testament. I hope to hear your answers, as they are the same responses I sought for all these writings.

Yours in Christ,

_____

November 24, 2008

Dear Holy Father,

I am sorely ashamed of the Roman Catholic Church hierarchy that insists on following the tradition of their predecessor's Eucharist, while paying lip service to the teaching's of Christ. Their deliberate deceit in distorting the new Covenant (Jer 31:31-34) in *Lumen Gentium* embarrasses so much that I hesitate to reveal the scandal by filing a lawsuit or distributing my writings to the public. Jesus said to the hierarchy of his day "How accurately Isaiah prophesied about you hypocrites . . ." (Mk 7:6), and it seems fitting today to describe your unloving in his prophetic words.

When I now pray that I believe in the "one holy catholic and apostolic Church" or "the holy catholic Church," it is the Church of Christ subsisting in the Catholic Church that I refer to. Plainly, you people in Rome, as well as my diocesan bishop, are out of light, and both your exclusive Eucharist and your *Dogmatic Constitution* (*Lumen Gentium*), as established and practiced in your Catholic Church, are plainly anti-Christ. In darkness, they expose you to judgment. But like a mother who took to prostitution, I still love my mother church from my youth. It is in her concern that I mainly write for the future.

If you are unaware of the wrongdoing, or if you are aware and dare not attempt to rectify the negation of God's saving action, you should be frightened. If you claim to be unaware of the wrong, read my letters, read my book, or talk to me. I may be the least of God's Catholics in what I prophesy, but I foresee the institutional Church strengthened for centuries by Constantine's advice in time, managed as are Mormons, Islam, and other worldly ruled churches. However, God's saving action has already occurred, in spite of any church, and your lording over Catholics in the long run will not substitute for God's imprints of Christ in each of us.

Yours concernedly,

_____

November 26, 2008

Dear Holy Father,

Aquinas used Aristotle's concept of instrumental cause to explain how God uses the Eucharist to communicate His grace to humans. The recipient may accordingly be in a state of sin or not spiritually disposed to cooperate with the grace contained in the Sacrament, but God still confers the graces *ex opera operato*. So, your rules of predisposition are mere tradition and unneeded according to this school of thought.

Aquinas drew his school of thought on his own experiences and upon scriptural and philosophical sources. When Canon lawyers legalized the Sacrament, and their rules became the norm, Aquinas' theology lost out. Still, the ordinary folk perceived the Sacrament as conferring grace automatically, no matter how distracted or unworthy the participants, because God chooses to grace us Himself. The Holy One anointed the faithful at Vatican II to espouse this universal Eucharist, but you choose to do it the traditionalist's way.

Vatican II's ressourcement to Christ's intent and possibly the imprinted beliefs of the entire body of the faithful anointed by the Holy One espouse an inclusive Eucharist of non-Catholics and sinners, as our New Testament scholars contended to you. As Father Joseph Ratzinger, you acknowledged this same idea (*God Is Near Us*, p. 59). But you had a conflict at the time and opposed the idea. You stated "—however tempting the idea may be—it contradicts what *we* find in the Bible" (Italics mine). Who are the conflicting "we" you referred to in 1968/9? Since your scriptural explanations (page 60, *Infra*) were so scripturally and scholarly wanting, I suspect this "we" had much to do with your rise in the hierarchy to your present position. I also submit that the idea's appeal was its truth, and you disputed it because it was in your self-interest to cling to the Church's traditional Eucharist and its fictions to gain your worldly goals.

Anthony Grafton pictured you as an academic rock star at work, "wielding proof texts that in his hand are as powerful, and as malleable, as articles of the Constitution in the hands of an ideological partisan jurist" (*The New Yorker*, 7/25/05). We saw this trait in action as you artfully made the criticized Church's Eucharist into what we have today. However, as Pope Benedict XVI, you remain empowered and obligated to use your talents to correct the Church's clear disregard of God's commandment of love, and you remain obligated to renew God's saving action towards humanity in its Church's Eucharist, as well as its *Dogmatic Constitution*. Christ awaits you to act or explain why you did not do his will on earth, and if you persist in the folly, may Christ have mercy on you.

Patiently yours,

_____

November 28, 2008

Dear Holy Father,

Stalag 17 was a movie about a German concentration camp holding an American solider whose wife writes him a letter announcing her pregnancy with his child. He has been incarcerated over a year, and on sharing the news with his fellow inmates, he keeps saying, "I believe. I believe." At times, I too find myself silently saying, "I believe. I believe" when I gaze upon Jesus Christ in the bread or cup used at Mass or when I accept the fact that Jesus Christ is God. If I disbelieved, I think I would quit writing to you.

Man or bread being God is a contradiction in terms and is unreasonable. Terms like transubstantiation, transfiguration, or the Word (*Logos*) being God in John's Prologue are logical, but only if you already have faith in Jesus Christ being Lord. Muslims, Jews, Albert Sweitzer, and many others do not have such faith, yet they hold Jesus in the highest esteem. You obviously upset Islam in 2006 by arguing that they should be more reasonable in regards to their faith, and recently you offered to discuss some Christian/Muslim understanding. You would do better by sharing Eucharist with them as Jesus ordered, because out of respect for him, they might consume the bread and allow Christ to transform them, just as in Aquinas/Aristotle's concept or *ex opera operato.*

God pledged to imprint in our minds and hearts how to know the unknowable God so effectively that the least knowable of us knows how to know God and His law of love. Without this assistance, we cannot know the mysteries of God. But from Jesus Christ's last words and actions, we try to believe that we too are to love each other as brothers and sisters in Christ. I believe based on God's assistance.

Jesus knew his scripture, and through life he progressed in learning how to know what God wanted of him. He believed that he was to be the paschal lamb (Ex 12), the suffering servant who gives himself up for "many" (Is 53) and performs God's covenant (Jer 31). Interdependent with his death, Jesus ordered the Eucharist memorial of God forgiving our sins and teaching His law of loving each other. At Emmaus, upon receiving the Eucharist, Cleopas' eyes opened to recognize Christ. Non-Catholics may need Eucharist for the heartfelt awakening to Christ. But where should they go?

With the belief God has imprinted the law of forgiveness in you and with the belief that Christ's excruciating love exemplified God's law of loving neighbors, why do you senselessly continue to exclude most of God's people from your Church or Eucharist? Where should we go?

Constantly inquiring, I am.

Sincerely,

———————————————

December 1, 2008

Dear Holy Father,

If you read any of my letters, you would realize that I read a lot of other people's experiences. I try to share them with you in order to touch your mind or heart on the common grounds of respecting the Eucharist. I just read the novel *River of Heaven*, by Lee Martin. Professor Martin writes of a homosexual who keeps his entire lonely life secret, from his condition to his involvement in the death of his gay sweetheart in their teenage years. You might appreciate reading about how withholding compassion or exercising cowardice to save oneself at the expense of others shapes our lives. Reading the memories of Martin's 70 year old hero can make you appreciate the lonely life of those you call abnormal, perverts, queers, or sinners—those who live closeted, without companionship or conformation to our prejudiced society. They suffer from perceiving heterosexual couples' happy lives even more than they suffer from the cruelties that most people heap on them.

My new diocesan Bishop, Jaime Soto, wrote in *Joy and Hope*, commending many who invested much in retaining the traditional definition of "marriage" of heterosexual couples, while depriving gays use of the term "marriage" for their partnerships—so much for giving others your shirt when they ask for your coat. Bishop Soto's commentary in *The Catholic Herald* affords me a view into his thinking, and when he attributes support for the traditional understanding of marriage to be a practice of charity, I see I have a new field I must plow. Charity is the fundamental Christian virtue of loving others, and the broader extent of ones love is the more correctly charitable one. Bishop Soto may have been absent the day Christ taught us this commandment of God.

Christ's invitation to our intimately loving union of sharing his body and blood occurred before his death and was voiced to his apostles. However, we know the words were interdependent with his self-sacrificed death and were meant for the whole world. It was meant for everyone to share with him today, in the same Sacrifice at Mass.

Yours in Christ,

_____

December 3, 2008

Dear Holy Father,

I succeeded in having a letter published in the *National Catholic Reporter* (see reverse page), hopefully in time to inform the Bishops in Synod on the separation of the Church from the teaching of Christ in concerning the New Covenant (Jer 31). In obedience to Church teachings, the bishops may be unaware of working toward an anti-Christ principle, an evil and a blasphemy against the Spirit, upon which the Catholic Church has not enlightened them.

Emeritus Bishop Remi de Roo of the dioceses of Victoria, Canada assured over 2000 Catholics at the November conference in Milwaukee that the spirit of the Second Vatican Council lives on strong. He pointed out that the enlightenment of *Lumen Gentium* still applies, especially that laypeople have the duty to speak up on concerns about the common good of the church. The gathering included laity enlightening us on how (1) church ministries are based "on the needs of the world," not "needs of the church" and (2) "We are going to take our church back," a "post-clerical" church (*NCR*, 11/28/08, p. 14).

Jesus accurately prophesied the hypocrisy of his own Jewish hierarchy (Mk 7:1-13) and our Catholic hierarchy today. The delay in getting a red hat for Giovanni Montini allowed Pope John XXIII to bring to light Vatican II's truths, but his untimely death also allowed the traditionalists to close ranks in Pope Paul VI, promulgating the distortions of *Lumen Gentium*, Ch. II, No. 9. Thus, the traditionalists returned us to the pre-council anti-Christ placement of the Catholic Church and into the shoes of the Fisherman. Instead of God's unilateral performance of salvation in Christ, the Roman Catholic Church becomes the "messianic people" and redeems the world. Mankind's tradition twisted God's gift of the New Covenant by turning to a bargain for exchange, securing the Catholic Church its worldly mission and power, instead of the free benefits gained by Christ's Cross.

As part and parcel of this anti-Christ conspiracy, Popes John Paul II and Benedict XVI were incompetent protagonists in rejecting the interpretations of Vatican II and the New Testament scholars' espousal of a universal Eucharist, wherein Christ's invitation to his supper was for a loving union of every human being. As a result, my Sacramento Diocese promulgated dogmatic statutes to bar non-Christians and others from Christ's open invitation. Based on anti-Christ ignorance, we cling to uncharitable traditions embodied in centuries of Catholic teaching. In doing so, Catholics enjoy the Eucharist without recognizing the universal body of Christ.

Caveat, (1 Cor 11:29)

Scripture synod

■ Your article on the Vatican scripture synod, "The Bible and the life of the church" (*NCR*, Oct. 31), reported the conflict between the mainstream view in recent Catholic scripture scholarship, holding to what the text meant in its original context versus late theological interpretations. I invite readers to read Jeremiah 31:33-34 in its context as a promise to the Israelites and then in its context at the Last Supper when Jesus explains its extension to all humanity. We hear it at Mass when the cup is raised and Jesus states that this is the Blood of the Covenant which is being shed for all.

Then read the distortion of the text in *Lumen Gentium*, Chapter II, No. 9, made by our theological interpretations. We delete from God's Covenant the main terms of the deal Christ fulfilled so dearly. For instance, God's pledge to "forgive their evildoing and remember their sin no more" is taken away. Thus Christ did not institute this pledge of salvation, nor does Christ alone teach us how to know God. Instead, we need the church to forgive our sins and to teach us that only Catholics are saved until we Catholics succeed in redeeming the human race.

FRED B. ITHURBURN
Yuba City, Calif.

December 5, 2008

Dear Holy Father,

Joseph Smith (another Joseph) founded the Church of Jesus Christ of Latter Day Saints (the Mormon Church) on his claim that God and Christ, Father and Son, descended from Heaven to reveal to him that since the time of Christ and the Apostles, Popes and those who claimed to be rightful interpreters of His truth led the world away from the true words and deeds of Jesus Christ. Smith contended he was the prophet assigned the Truth's Restoration (*The 19th Wife*, p. 47, by David Ebershoff). His Church centered on love, "love begets love," and has had success in growing a number of disciplined adherents who aim to spread Christ's love message to all of mankind.

Lumen Gentium's Ch. II, No. 9 lays claim for Catholics as "those who believe in Christ," being the messianic people established by Christ for the redemption of the whole world. However, it is the Church of Christ that His blood purchases for the whole world, and He fills it with his Spirit. By means of the Eucharistic sacrifice, we offer ourselves with Christ, the victim, to God, and we manifest our unity by the offering and through Holy Communion. On the surface, among the differences between us and the Mormon Church appears to be their nonacceptance of the Trinity or the Eucharist as part of God's plan for redemption of the whole world.

Apparently, neither religion accepts that God alone has already saved each and every one of us, or that God has taught us how to know Love through Jesus Christ's words, deeds, and His ratification and institution of the New Covenant in His testament. God's agreement, performed by Christ in his blood, pledges that "no longer will they have need to teach their friends and kinsmen how to know the Lord" (Jer 31:34). God also pledges that "All . . . *shall* know me . . ." (Italics mine). So, neither Church's teachings are needed, both are probably superfluous. However, the edifices in Rome and Salt Lake City stand to diminish God's teachings as acceptable from the filthy wooden Cross at Calvary, and their illustriousness insures that truth-tellers, such as me, will make no impact on those who treasure them.

So, as ordered by Jesus Christ, the Eucharistic sacrifices retain the Cross as the essential memorial teachings of words and deeds of God on earth. A universal Holy Communion teaches a loving relationship between God and all humanity as God intends. Consider that, while announcing grape juice would be used at all communion stations, the Mormon's gay service, at page 315 of *The 19th Wife*, quoted the following, "The one who comes to me, I will certainly not cast out" (John 6:37). I submit that if it was a Mass for all people, it would please Christ more.

Amusingly yours,

———————————————

December 8, 2008

Dear Holy Father,

Friday, my pastor asked the congregation to define "faith." He referred to a faith that healed a couple of blind men at Jesus Christ's hands. However, the concept of faith is more than what Father Francisco may have had in mind. For instance, most of those at Mass were elementary grade students, and many there had faith in the existence of Santa Claus. The acuteness of the concept of faith increases when we accept Jesus Christ, or when we accept Father holding a piece of bread, which Jesus says "is my body." Thomas Acquina squeezed "transubstantiation" out of Aristotelian logic, and it comforted the Council of Trent. But, it still runs contrary to the reality of bread as God or as man. It takes the faith of little children, and by that means, God imprints in our hearts how to know Him and His law of love. From conception and by heart, we know these matters which God causes us to know in the Blood of the Covenant, but no way could I define this faith to Father.

God pledged that "all from the least to the greatest" shall know how to know, so that we need no Church to teach us (Jer 31:33-34). Jesus, as God, could truthfully state that he was bread or wine, and by sacrificing himself on the Cross, he perfected humanity of its defects, making it One with him forever. God, through Jesus Christ, did this for us out of goodness, and not out of our faith or any merits separate from God's performance of the unilateral agreement of teaching and forgiving us all.

I write mainly to you for your understanding because you, unlike the Catholic Church, have the competency to understand lectures and sermons, as evidenced by your past writings. By the same expertise, you know better than what you are practicing, and I ask: Do you appreciate the extent of your wrongdoing, and do you have the moral courage to overcome your conduct? In Ch. II, No. 9 *Lumen Gentium* plainly spells out the Church's anti-Christ negation of God's saving action in scriptural history. Your personal contribution to the anti-Christ conspiracy contradicts our New Testament scholars contention for an inclusive Eucharist, and, though feeling the idea to be "tempting" (which I suggest was the Spirit's contact), you argued like an ideologically partisan Catholic for the traditionalists' exclusive Eucharist and wielded strained interpretations of Bible and the *Didache* as God's qualification of God's law of love (*God Is Near Us*, pp. 59-60).

Peace is in our children and in most people thanks to Christ and his angels at Bethlehem. But, God meant for the Eucharist to also assure us of His love for us so that we, in peace, would respond with love. The conspiracy of silence that you and my spiritual leaders practice in response to my writings evidences that lack of fatherly love that you conduct. Am I disturbing your peace of mind?

Peacefully Yours,

_____

Dear Holy Father,

Jesus Christ evidenced God's saving action in history by dying to establish the New and Everlasting Covenant (Mk 14:24). The terms of that God-formed-covenant were spelled out to the Israelites as pledges by God and promised to God's people. God was to unilaterally perform the agreement in days to come (Jer 31:31-34).

Jesus expressly ratified and instituted the New Covenant—the New Testament—in his Blood (*cf.* 1 Cor 11:25), making all humanity one in the Spirit. These became the new People of God, who by heart knew how to know our God of love, "for I will forgive their evildoing and remember their sin no more" (Jer 3:34). The days God forecasted have come with Christianity.

Jesus Christ also fulfilled God's pledge to teach all of us, from least to greatest, how to know the Lord and His Law of love. Thus, we no longer need anyone other than Christ to teach us these truths. Jesus learned from experience and increased in wisdom and human knowledge, but He depended on faith, ignorance, and superstitions on matters that He was not called on to reveal. On matters He was inspired to reveal, He may have spoke as instructed (Jn 12:49, 50).

However, Jesus took pains to reveal that He died to establish the New Covenant as the rule of God's kingdom on earth. A new age and a new People of God were created at the moment of Jesus' death, and in their innocence, they were recreated in how to know God in the love Jesus showed them. Thus, God evidenced his saving action of humanity in the history of the Passion and Cross.

He loved us just as He created us—prone to sinning—and in Jesus Christ's sacrifice, He gave us the Eucharist as a memorial gift with no strings attached to know, love, and serve everyone.

John XXIII's death freed the Catholic hierarchy to promulgate *Lumen Gentium*, Ch. II, No. 9's contradiction of the teaching of Jesus by deleting the New Covenant's pledges, such as, "for I will forgive," etc.

(see above). The hierarchy again usurps Christ as Savior and replaces Him with the messianic Catholics who supposedly will redeem the world someday. Though promulgated by Pope Paul VI, this may be both blasphemy and an anti-Christ negation of God's saving Gospel, thusly nullifying on paper God's law of love today.

The Church of Christ subsists in the Catholic Church, but not when it excludes most of the People of God from the Church or its Holy Communion. In your doctoral dissertation, you wrote that true Church could not uncharitably exclude others from sacraments. Before the public catches on, I suggest that we rid ourselves of our blasphemy and invite everyone to the Lord's Supper as Christ intended to occur in order to do the will of God.

Yours in love,

_____

December 12, 2008

Dear Holy Father,

I was informed that you stated that the Our Father prayer's "give us this day our daily bread" refers to the Bread of Christ that we receive at Holy Communion. Since I will not be aware of your response to the statement, let us assume that this is your opinion and discuss it in my monologue. As a child, I thought it referred to the life-giving sustenance that poor children sought daily, but as I aged, I felt it was more about the nourishment that Jesus said he received to do the will of his Father at the Samaritan's well.

Your contention may be reasonable in light of the prayer being said in common with all people of "Our Father." Then again, you directed a limitation for only Catholic use of the Church's Eucharist, and a special request of God to furnish daily Eucharist for Catholics cleansed by both Christ and Church seems like over-gilding the lilies.

Pope John XXIII and the bishops in council exercised ressourcement by imitating Christ in Spirit when they espoused a global Church of Christ, with all created peoples making up the members. Thus, an inclusive Eucharist, as Christ ordered for all, was espoused so that His redemption and salvation would be carried with and to everyone in order to transform humanity. But, as Father Bernard Haring wrote of you and Karol Wojtyla, you persuaded others to modify Vatican II's principles and restrict their interpretations back to pre-council traditions. *Lumen Gentium* and the Church's exclusive Eucharist are fruits of what you and the boys in Rome planted. Your book, *God Is Near Us*, on the Eucharist proves your own contribution to our anti-Christ Church Eucharist. On pages 59 and 60 you leave most of the world to be harmed by your exclusive Eucharist opinion, which metastasized to include my Diocese.

In today's Gospel, Elizabeth's filled Spirit cries to Mary, "Blessed are you who believed that what was spoken to you by the Lord would be fulfilled." I pray that the Holy Spirit will have you believe that Christ has fulfilled in everyone what God pledged to all of us in the Blood of the New and Everlasting Covenant. To wit, God forgives and forgets our evildoing. So enlightened you will see that everyone must be invited to share Holy Communion with us on Jesus' order.

Concernedly yours,

_____

Fred Ithurburn

December 15, 2008

Dear Holy Father,

My December 8 letter mentioned Aquinas and his Aristotelian metaphysics, which gave us "transubstantiation" to explain Jesus Christ in the bread used at Mass. You argued that the Church's members' common participation in the Eucharist defines the true Church, and using the Thomistic definition, you justified the exclusion of politicians who defend abortion rights from the Eucharist. You used the noun *substantia*, meaning substance or the essence of the true Church (as in the Body in bread's "transubstantiation"), to relate to *Lumen Gentium*'s verb *subsists*, and as in the Church of Christ subsists in the Catholic Church (Ch. 1, No. 8). In 1964 you wrote a book on being enthusiastic on the new openness in Vatican II's Church's description, but in 1984 you changed and narrowed the Church of Christ's definition, excluding non-Catholics in favor of conforming to the traditionalists in Rome. You strongly argued that "subsists" identifies Christ's Church in strongest terms as "both is, and can only be, *fully* present" (emphasis added) in the Roman Church, with all its hierarchies (*The New Yorker*, 7/25/05, p. 42).

What if the post-Vatican II scholars of the New Testament were correct in 1968? It was an idea you then found "tempting"—that Christ meant for all created people, sinners and non-Catholics included, to be invited to his Lord's Supper (*God Is Near Us*, p. 59). Then, would the members' common participation in the Eucharist prove them to be People of God and thusly necessary members of the Church of Christ, the true Church, which subsists in the Roman Catholic Church? Parenthetically, as you wrote in your doctorial dissertation, St. Augustine would argue that the Catholic Church would be true Church since it excludes no member from the Sacrament.

With the Diocese of Sacramento's Diocesan Statutes of the Third Diocesan Synod's exclusion of non-Christians and others from the reception of Holy Communion: it is not Christ's Church. It is an anti-Christ action. It states blasphemy against the Holy Spirit, and it is in plain violation of God's Commandment to love our neighbors as ourselves. This gnat was squeezed out in 2006.

Open to Fatherly advice,

December 15, 2008

Dear Holy Father,

By copy of this letter, I am corresponding (if monologues are included) with my Godson/Nephew, Jim Forgarty. Jim is a brother in mission with Brothers and Sisters in Love who serve the inner city poor of Chicago. Religious purchased him a silver colored cassock to wear for purposes of self-preservation when he waded among his members to break up gang wars. He has survived 25 years of this occupation, and his clothing may have contributed to his life's work.

Since Jim attends many funerals, prisons, and places needing to hear, I want to share some thoughts that you refuse to consider of importance and refuse to tell the world with fatherly advice. The sinners and poor that Jesus especially served are those to whom Jim gives his life and, hopefully, will share this story. Today, the Entrance Antiphon, from Jeremiah and Isaiah, announced, "Nations hear the message of the Lord, and make it known to the ends of the earth: Our Savior is coming. Have no fear." The Angels also heralded the Glorified Jesus' greetings, "Peace be with you," which all should hear.

People should know what the Churches refuse to announce—Jesus Christ's death extended peace to every created person via the New Covenant pledges of God (Jer 31, Mk 14:24, and Lk 20:22). This good news is that God forgives everyone of their evildoing and teaches everyone, even the least of humans, how to know Him and by heart know God's law of love. Although the Covenant rids us of need for any teacher other than Christ, Churches insist on teaching their own versions and fear-mongering for their self-importance. Christ is our only teacher.

Christ, our savior, redeemed the world, and this includes every person that Jim will ever meet. Each one need fear no vice, no sin, no hell, no Satan, and no danger, because God loves them as they are. Through Jesus Christ, we each are made One with Him at conception. Of course, we should reciprocate for what Jesus purchased for us so dearly, but Jesus Christ alone will judge and chastise us if his redemption is found wanting. So, don't fear and be at peace. We have it made. We need only the Eucharist to thank and embrace Christ. That is the purpose of the Catholic Church—to serve the Eucharistic sacrifice to everybody, with no strings attached.

Joyfully yours,

_____

December 17, 2008

Dear Holy Father,

Yesterday's Opening Prayer at Mass reminded us, "Father of Love, you made a new creation through Jesus Christ, your son. May his coming free us from sin and renew his life within us . . . ." I don't know who initially prayed thus, but in Advent, the prayer fits the season of Christ's coming from millennia ago and accompanying us since.

It brings to mind Jesus saying "I solemnly assure you, history has not known a man born of woman greater than John the Baptizer. Yet the least born into the kingdom of God is greater than he" (Mt 11:11). By Jesus' death, a recreation of humanity apparently occurred in the Blood of the Covenant. Thereby, even the least of us born into Christ's Kingdom is baptized in the Spirit and Blood of the Crucified Lord. God thereby constantly forgives our evildoing, and the least of us is taught and is born greater in Spirit than John the Baptist. Metaphysically, we might add that we are born even greater than the angels.

"The son of Man has come to search out and save what is lost" (Lk 19:10) assures us that Christ's crucifixion redeemed the world. The last will and testament of Jesus fulfilled the purification of each and every one of us. Plus, we all inherited the common parent of Jesus Christ. The Roman Catholic Church, however, uncharitably redrafted the Covenant or Testament to delete God's pledges and soiled what God made clear in Christ's redemption. By claiming, in *Lumen Gentium*, Ch. II, No. 9, that only believers in Christ are the new creation and that all others must await redemption by the messianic people, man nullifies God's Covenant.

Must we again hear a voice state "What God has purified you are not to call unclean" (Acts 10:15) to show you, like Peter, that God shows no partiality? God pledged that everyone's sins would be forgiven and forgotten in the excruciating death of Jesus. Thus, God purified the habitual sinner to be worthy enough to receive Holy Communion. As for bringing judgment upon himself for receiving Eucharist while in mortal sin, Jesus Christ will deal with his chastisement, if any, in the hereafter.

Yours open for correction,

_____

December 19, 2008

Dear Holy Father,

Please read this poem, "Love" by George Herbert (1593-1633), in regard to a universal Eucharist:

> Love bade me welcome; yet my soul drew
>   back,
>   Guilty of dust and sin.
> But quick-ey'd Love, observing me grow
>   slack
>   From my first entrance in,
> Drew nearer to me, sweetly questioning
>   If I lack'd anything.

"A guest," I answered, "worthy to be here."
    Love said, "You shall be he."
"I the unkind, ungrateful? Ah my dear,
    I cannot look on thee."
Love took my hand, and smiling did reply,
    "Who made the eyes but I?"

Truth, Lord, but I have marr'd them; let
    my shame
    Go where it doth deserve."
"And know you not, says Love, "who bore
    the blame?"
    "My dear, then I will serve."
"You must sit down," says Love, "and taste
    my meat."
    So I did sit and eat.

                                 Yours in Love,

December 22, 2008

Dear Holy Father,

It is the healers, such as Christ, who are remembered for teaching us to live beyond the limitations of our self-love. In his suffering and death, Christ, the healer, taught us the way to improve the world to real earthly peace and mutual care. He died to teach us God's covenant of loving everyone on earth as equal people of God.

A non-believer and one you would never invite as worthy to your Church's Eucharist is Albert Sweitzer, who healed non-Christians of Africa. He healed by deed and was of good character, believing Jesus was not God. But as a healer and lover of humans in general, those of us who knew him remember him with love. Sweitzer would be disqualified by our Church as a non-believer in Christ, and he died without the messianic Catholic people redeeming him. Had he taken the Eucharist, which his mentor Jesus told him to take, God could have more clearly imprinted the actual presence of Himself in his heart, confirming Sweitzer's rightness in his impartial loving of everyone. Through Holy Communion, the peace that he sought would be with him more than it already was. God would imprint in his mind and heart that the actual Jesus was also in those he helped on earth, as he most likely knows today.

You, who have the ear of the world, heal and supposedly love humanity just as Christ loves. Christ made us all one to live in peace and love each other. So, everybody is everyone. You lectured that serving "for many" (Mk 14:24) prevents the Catholic Church from becoming a select community of the righteous (*Commonweal*, 4/21/06). However, you now sit as leader of a Catholic Church that condemns to perdition all those who do not "believe in Christ" (*Lumen Gentium*). As Joseph Ratzinger, you taught, preached, and wrote of your faith convictions to establish that Christ redeemed the world. Today, you reign with an anti-Christ constitution and Eucharist.

You, who read this letter, have more ability to catch the attention of Pope Benedict XVI. I urge you; pray that he have the courage of his faith convictions. In our nothingness, we need the Holy Spirit to imprint in us all how to love others as we love Catholics.

Yours in Christ,

_____

December 24, 2008

Dear Holy Father,

Some regard Barack Obama "like a rock star," and as the Beatles songs moved the world, so too may his ideas on religious history move the world. He is an American politician, but his popularity has magnetism much broader and may come to affect worldviews for years to come. In short, I forecast that he will be a religious force in the Church of Christ that will embrace all peoples and all faith convictions on earth.

My letters to you about a universal Eucharist concern the common good of the Catholic Church. I hereby caution that you should reckon with the religious force that the American people have and will have on the world's scene. God, fully knowledgeable of human history from Alpha to Omega, designed His saving action of humankind as Jesus Christ, in his Last Supper, spelled out words interdependent with his death on Calvary. As a result, everyone is free of everlasting death, and we are all one in Christ's loving, forever. Unfortunately, Catholics' misunderstandings of what God imprinted in our hearts of how to know the Lord of love and God's law of love negated both the Lord's teachings of love and the fact that we are forgiven to be forever with Christ in love. God perceived this would happen, and He gave us the Eucharist.

The epilogue of the *Selected Writings of Jose Miguel de Barandiaran: Basque Prehistory and Ethnography* probates the above as it reads, "now that the Basques are being faced with new modes of economic, social, and political life, they seem also to be disconcerting themselves from the Christian ideal and elaborating a new world of representations, a new concept of life associated with these new ways, relegating the old values to the marginal zones of their existence" (Page 118).

Being full-blooded Basque, I was thrilled when I discovered that Jesus Christ established the New Covenant in his blood (Jer 31:33–34), which informed me that I was free of fear of sinning as I was forgiven of whatever evildoing I persisted in. Christ thereby taught me to know by heart that God loved me as I was and that God would imprint in my conscience how to know Him and His law of loving others. Basques, in general, love freedom from human rules but will enthusiastically accept the new concept of life that Christ gave them in the New Covenant with no strings attached.

Shalom,

———————————————

December 26, 2008

Dear Holy Father,

Human history shows that our learning evolves exponentially. Vatican II was a sensible moment which attempted to bring Catholicism up to speed with the global Christianity that Jesus Christ established in God's Covenant. His Eucharist supposedly constantly redeems humankind on earth, but the failing of man to understand resulted in the need of the Catholic Church to admit its failings and attempt a ressourcement to identify itself with the Church of Christ. Both you and Han Kung, with later liberation theologians, questioned making the synoptic Gospel's historical Jesus the canonical criterion for all subsequent church failings. You saw the Catholic Church as a bride who has not always lived up to her calling. In other words, the Church is a company of sinners involved in fanaticism, self-alienation, and human degradation. In 1968/9, you put it bluntly, "The institutional church does not coincide with the church's essence" (*Commonweal*, 4/21/06).

The university students in Tübingen disturbed you. At the time, our youth in the USA largely rejected organized religion, and these peers of the Catholic youth influenced them to be less orthodox. This trend of acquiring culture, and perhaps theology, from expanding modern enlightenment and media technology (the Beatles worldwide impact is an example) continues and will likely keep continuing.

I suspect that your conversion to join the traditionalists in 1968/9 manifested when you contradicted Vatican II's contention for a universal Eucharist (*God Is Near Us*, p.59). Confirming your change of faith, in 2005 you argued that the Council used the phrase that the true Church of Christ "subsists" (*Lumen Gentium*, Ch. I, No. 8) in its strongest terms, to mean it "both is, and can only be, <u>fully</u> present in the Roman Church . . ." (*The New Yorker*, 7/25/05, p. 42). In 1964, K. Wojtyla persuaded Pope Paul VI to promulgate the distortion of the New Covenant (Jer 31:33–34) in *Lumen Gentium*, Ch. II, No. 9. In the half century since, you and Pope John Paul II, both protagonists who continue to persuade us to your restrictive interpretations of Vatican II, protected the post-Vatican II modifications from divulgence. By the same pact of restrictions, no one answers my letters.

However, the trend to know the truth will beat out the deceits in time. Tell me then where will you have put Catholic credibility? I submit that you nullified, negated, and buried Our Lord's pledges, and you preach an uncharitable faith, as spelled out in the New Covenant.

Yours in Christ,

December 29, 2008

Dear Holy Father,

I make little of the courage you would be asked to have to reverse the Dogmatic Constitution on the Church so that the messianic people would include the whole human race, who needs not await their redemption by us chosen ones because Christ already redeemed the world. Specifically, change *Lumen Gentium*'s Ch. II, No. 9, which makes only those who believe in Christ, those who are now the people of God, the people to be reborn as a chosen race.

I read a novel written by Luis Miguel Rocha, a television writer and producer, entitled *The Last Pope*. It is a story about Albino Luciani, who died as John Paul I a mere thirty three (33) days after his election to the office you hold. According to the story, members high in the Curia or hierarchy executed him because he jeopardized their standing and threatened the Church with a financial scandal that would damage its reputation. Of course, it is fiction, but it dawned on me that what we ask of you—to return the Roman Catholic Church to the Eucharist and the community of servants that Jesus Christ intended—would wipe out far more treasures the Curia gained than those who Rocha imagined in his writings. Still, the spirit of the Inquisitors lives on in the Church, not only threatening you, but ending this monologue at either end of its postage if the establishment feels threatened.

Assuming you imagine similar risks to yourself as in the story above, you should invite them. Be a martyr and lessen any chastisement you earn for sins. Besides, at our ages, we have less to be concerned about self-aggrandizing than we do about facing Our Lord with our judgments. In my studies, I discern an anti-Christ concern for the good of the Church. I may express erroneous opinions on the things I write to you. I may sin in violating the teachings as Bishop William Wiegand wrote to me in August 2007. However, your silence to my correspondence, if not caused by those in Rome who keep you from responding, tells me I may be right. God's commandment of loving others dictates that I should continue my efforts.

Others who read my letters may leave it up to me to sound off, because they have more to fear from discipline in the Church than I do. There are those who urge me to continue writing even though they believe my ends are impossible to obtain.

Yours in Christ,

_____

Dear Holy Father,

Recall in our youth that we were forbidden to read the Bible, and in "obedience of faith," we were to accept the teaching of the Church instead. Apparently, the authors of *Lumen Gentium*, Ch. II, No. 9 still cling to that tradition, negating God's commandment to impartially love everyone. The Bible belies their efforts, as we hear at Mass how Jesus bled to death to fulfill God's New Covenant. He and we know how to know the Lord and His law (Jer 31:33–34).

Pope Pius XII called on us to study the Bible in 1943 in order to undercut Catholic fundamentalism. He also urged us to promote democracy by stating that, "the future belongs to democracy." In 1944, his Christmas radio message spoke from WWII experience, "Taught by bitter experience, people today more and more oppose monopolies of power that are dictatorial, accountable to no one, and impossible to reject. They want a system of government more compatible with the dignity and liberty due citizens." Pius XII obviously influenced Vatican II. John XXIII tried to follow suit, but he died an untimely death.

Pope Paul VI and the Curia reasserted control in time to author 1964's *Lumen Gentium*. Still, in 1968/9 you experienced student rebellions and disruptions in the Church, such as plummeting vocations and empty pews. You traditionalists attributed that to unexpected consequences of the assembled bishops and their espoused openness. New Testament scholars, still in the Spirit of Vatican II, contended that Christ meant for an open Eucharist, where non-Catholics and sinners unconditionally shared.

Confronted by these New Testament scholars' *caritas*, the students' rejection of the orthodox, and the supposedly unintended consequences of Vatican II, you joined the Traditionalists in power to insist on continuing their teachings of Catholic Church: exclusion over inclusion, ruling over serving, monarchy over democracy, and (to my sorrow) monologue over dialogue. Jesus so aptly prophesied the hypocrisy of such People clinging to human traditions and disregarding

God's commandment to love each other impartially and democratically (Mk 7:1–13). Thus, we have our anti-Christ Eucharist.

God foresees how we evolve, and He designs our saving action in history to be by Christ's sacrifices on the Cross. In Christ's sacrifices of the Eucharist, everyone transforms to God's love throughout the whole world. You personally must know these truths and appreciate that you must return us to the democracy of shared love, because even the least of us knows tis self-evident truth by heart (Jer 31:33–34, Mk 14:24). If you won't, we will obey Christ in *caritas*.

Yours in Christ,

_____

December 31, 2008

Dear Holy Father,

Politically, our Religious Left in the USA reclaimed its place based upon the more open-minded citizens' religious ideas. Barack Obama caught this drift and succeeded in his campaign for the presidency. Unfortunately, the openness clashes with the Catholic faithful who reject a woman's right to choose an abortion and a gay's claim to equal rights in coupling, painting them both as nonbelievers to be excluded from our Church and our Eucharist. "Openness," however, calls for mercy and love.

For all believers and nonbelievers, Christ secured forgiveness of any evildoing and a forgotten status for their sins by establishing the New Covenant in His Blood. Hereafter, the Lord judges, not us. So, the Blood of the Covenant makes all involved in abortions and abnormal sexual activities worthy of receiving Holy Communion. They are worthy simply because God purifies them, even when they are continuing the sinful life.

American youth largely reject organized religion because man-made rules are added to the Covenant. These people influence Catholics to be more unorthodox. Many globally acquire their theology from emulating our youths' social lives, while inventive youth and the expanding media influence the whole world. God foresaw this from the beginning. His plan of salvation is in Jesus Christ's redemption of the world, fulfilling God's New Covenant. God succeeds in loving and forgiving us today, while the Catholic Church's work redemption idea fails. *Lumen Gentium* alters the terms of Christ's last will and testament to insert Catholics in Christ's place of redeeming non-Catholics, which is non-effective because God redeems the world. Like Christ said to Peter, "Get out of my sight you Satan! You are trying to make me trip and fall" (Mt 16:21 *ff*).

So, as our Vicar of Christ, please remedy the situation and return the Catholic Church to the ressourcement that Vatican II started. Return us to God's saving action in history, where we know that Christ forgives every evildoing, and through his death and sharing of the Eucharist, He teaches the world how to know that God loves us. Thereby, all humanity may proclaim the mystery of faith that Jesus' death and resurrection lovingly saves the world. Christ Himself convinces those who hear that He set everyone free to sin or love as their hearts choose. When they know how excruciating his dying for us out of love was, few may choose to sin. Many may freely love in reciprocation. This may be the love they learn from Christ, which God planned when he willfully created us.

You all may disagree, but I discern from my informed conscience, mind, or heart that the mystery evidences this as God's saving action in history. It is God's unilateral Covenant at work. Leave it to God to make good on the Covenant through Christ's efforts. Careful! Do not get in Christ's way by teaching and performing a distorted Covenant. As Peter was told, "You are not judging by God's standards but by man's" (Mt 16:23). The Catholic way seemingly is anti-Christ.

Yours open for discussion,

———————————————

January 2, 2009

Dear Holy Father,

Both you and I believe that ". . . the blood of the covenant to be poured out on behalf of many" (Mk 14:24) prevents the Church from becoming a select community of the righteous, a community that condemns the wayward masses to perdition. Or so reported your student from the winter semester of 1968/69, Professor Ronald Modras, using his 152 page typescript of your opinions. Accordingly, you believe this (1) based on Jesus preaching to the "lost sheep of Israel" (Mt 10:5) and (2) based on Jesus not intending to found a church (*Commonweal*, 4/21/06, 12 *ff*).

However, purportedly speaking for Vatican II in 1964, *Lumen Gentium* stated that this sacred council teaches, "Whoever, therefore, knowing that the Catholic Church was made necessary by Christ, would refuse to enter or remain in it, could not be saved" (Ch. II, No. 14). Thus, the Church claimed to reject people saved by Christ from salvation, which you taught was prevented by Mark's quote, "for many." I argue that "the covenant" benefit saves even those who willfully choose not to be Catholics.

May 1971's *St. Anthony's Messenger* reported on pages 47–48 that Father Raymond Brown, our accepted expert on the Bible, stated, "I do not believe the demons inhabit desert places or the upper air, as Jesus and Paul thought . . . I see no way to get around the difficulty except by saying that Jesus and Paul were wrong on this point. They accepted the beliefs of their times about demons, but those beliefs were superstitious." I would argue with you that in those telling last hours Jesus spoke as instructed by God, establishing the Covenant benefits. By the Cross, Jesus Christ redeemed the world.

Pope Paul VI and the authors' of *Lumen Gentium*'s sentiments irreverently contradict Jesus' last words, which plainly assert his intent to perform God's New and Everlasting Covenant for everyone. In Christ's covenant, God pledged to unconditionally save everybody. Thereby, God's covenant and law of love saved the People of God, inclusive of every human—baptized or not. Only those clinging to pre-Vatican II traditions agree with this Dogmatic Constitution on the Church, something so blatantly uncharitable and self-serving that it contends that Christ failed to perform the Covenant perfectly. It also contends that God reneged on the pledge to forgive and forget our evildoing, while redeeming less than all of humanity.

Like Father Brown, you may find it difficult to call the Church wrong, but in 1968/9, you correctly lectured that Christ's Cross, not a church, redeems the world. Now, you must cure our Church of its Donatist-like wrongs and its anti-Christ Eucharist. My hope rests on you because of your learned mind, and I pray that your successor will find that you used it to correct the Church's wrongdoing.

Yours in Christ,

January 5, 2009

Dear Holy Father,

The Christmas day Mass had a reading from John's Prologue that caught my attention. It referred to those Christ empowered to become children of God:

> These are they who believe in his name — who were begotten not by blood nor by man's willing it, but by God.

Christ's fulfillment of the New Covenant pledges of God begets the people of God. Clearly, God unilaterally performs the deal through the Triune presence and not "by man's willing it, but by God." So, those who believe in his name believe because of Jesus Christ's fulfillment of their knowledge through his death and resurrection, carrying our unbelief onto the Cross with our sins.

Christ's testamentary will probates in heaven and on earth, specifically in the hearts of his heirs, who include every human being born to the kingdom established that first Easter. Determining the validity of Christ's will does not depend on the Catholic Church, and the modification of the terms of Christ's testament in *Lumen Gentium* is wrong in jurisprudence and plainly is against Christ's will. However, with the authority of Matthew's interpretations (Mt 16:19 or 18:18) and adding a questionable and unstable Pope IX's claim of infallibility, the Church apparently rejects the pledge of God's saving action in history and nullifies Christ's loving evidence of redemption.

With the Diocesan Statute of 2006 and Bishop Wiegand's August 2007 letter stating his opinion that I merely need "obedience of faith" to accept the teachings of the Church, my local spiritual leaders leave me concerned. However, until Bishop Jaime Soto responds, my hopes remain with His Holiness Pope Benedict XVI to be awakened by the Spirit of Christ. It is within you to do what you know you should do, such as amending *Sacramentum Caritatis* and personally feeding Christ's sheep. God forgives our evildoing, but negating God's saving actions is a blasphemy against the Spirit that may not be forgiven (Mt 12:31 *ff*).

Meanwhile, from my nothingness I will continue to write to remedy the wrong that I perceive my Catholic Church persists in under boot-strapping auspices. Perhaps it takes a sinner to better discover another's sins. If so, I qualify and obligatorily charge that the Church's exclusive Eucharist is a sin practiced against God's main commandment, to wit, the love of neighbor as oneself.

Yours in Christ,

_____

Fred Ithurburn

January 7, 2009

Dear Holy Father,

Covenanted to people, God delivers on his promises in the performance of Christ onto and on His Cross. For my service of Holy Communion, the *Prayer for Communion* furnished me to the convalescent fits of God's unilateral performance, which accomplished salvation:

> God our Father,
> You have called us to share the one bread
>   and one cup
> and so become one in Christ.
> Help us to live in him
> that we may bear fruit,
> *rejoicing that he has redeemed the world.*
> We ask this through Christ our Lord. (Italics mine)

God created us with free will, and He knows we will sin. But, we might also love others than ourselves. So, God intended for Christ's love to reveal God and His commandment of love, a God/Christ saving action in our history. That is news to be shared in Eucharistic sacrifices everywhere.

But like unsatisfied spouses, we met Constantine and were seduced into accepting his comforts in exchange for us succumbing to his idea of unity based on a creed discipline. Because of John and his community at Ephesus, we were ready to adopt "belief" as our criterion of faith, rather than Christ's words and actions that established God's covenant. And that covenant saves us regardless of belief, creed, or church. Note that the Fourth Gospel and *Lumen Gentium* fail to mention the Synoptic's covenant truths.

If any one of you readers appreciates these thoughts, His Holiness Pope Benedict XVI taught these same sentiments before his elevation.

He appreciates the anti-Christ sentiments of those who fabricated the law of *Lumen Gentium*, Ch. II, No. 9, changing the New and Everlasting Covenant that Jesus Christ established. However, we should pray for the Holy Father's moral courage, or we should pray against whatever wants to delay his performance. I suggest that he needs both our help and certainly an effort from the Holy Spirit to awaken his mind and heart to carry out Christ's aims. I also think that since he once found it "tempting" (p. 59, *God Is Near Us*) to follow the post-Vatican II New Testament scholars' idea that Christ meant for an unconditionally open Eucharist, Pope Benedict XVI will follow his heart and open our Church's Eucharist to invite everyone alive.

Yours in Christ,

——————————————

January 9, 2009

Dear Holy Father,

On the reverse page I copied pages 18 and 19 of No. 9, Ch. II of *Lumen Gentium* to follow up on my last letter to you. The copy on the reverse page shows the liberties taken by the scribes in misquoting the New Covenant of Jer 31:31–34 from the New Catholic Edition of the Holy Bible (Douay Version of The Old Testament). For example, Verse 34 actually reads as follows:

> 34. And they shall teach no more every man his neighbor, and every man his brother, saying: Know the Lord, for all shall know me from the least of them even to the greatest, saith the Lord: for I will forgive their iniquity, and I will remember their sin no more.

In drafting the Dogmatic Constitution on the Church, the Roman Catholic Church dares to reword God's New and Everlasting Covenant. It deletes God's pledge to forgive and forget our sins, and it amends

Christ's last testament, erasing benefits to every individual for which Christ shed his last drop of blood. For mankind, Christ purchased relief from death.

Also, the Catholic hierarchy attempts to delete the benefit that God pledged to imprint within us—how to know God and His law of love. The hierarchy tries to teach us its own version of salvation. But, God teaches, so everybody knows by heart that this Catholic Church lacks the fundamental virtue of charity when denying His benefits to non-Catholics. It cannot be true to the Church of Christ when it is founded upon the exclusion of our neighbors. Plainly, you are called to reverse this anti-Christ clinging to tradition and return us to the way Christ teaches—to love everyone.

Open for Discussion,

Chapter II

On the People of God

9. At all times and in every race God has given welcome to whoever fears him and does what is right (cf. Acts 10:35). God, however, does not make men holy and save them merely as individuals, without bond or link between one another. Rather has it pleased him to bring men together as one people, a people which acknowledges him in truth and serves him in holiness. He therefore chose the race of Israel as a people unto himself. With it he set up a covenant. Step by step he taught and prepared this people, making known in its history both himself and the decree of his will and making it holy unto himself. All these things, however, were done by way of preparation and as a figure of that new and perfect covenant, which was to be ratified in Christ, and of that fuller revelation which was to be given through the Word of God himself made flesh.*"Behold the days shall come says the Lord, and I will make a new covenant with the House of Israel, and with the house of Judah.... I will give my law in their bowels, and I will write it in their heart, and I will be their God, and they shall be my people.... For all of them shall know me, from the least of them even to the greatest, says the Lord" (Jer 31:31-34). Christ instituted this New Covenant, the New Testament, that is to say, in his Blood (cf. 1 Cor 11:25), calling together a people made up of Jew and Gentile, making them one, not according to the flesh but in the Spirit. This was to be the new People of God. For those who believe in Christ, who are reborn not from a perishable but from an imperishable seed

*Emphasis mine

through the word of the living God (cf. 1 Pt 1:23), not from the flesh but from water and the Holy Spirit (cf. Jn 3:5-6), are finally established as "a chosen race, a royal priesthood, a holy nation, a purchased people...who in times past were not a people, but are now the people of God" (1 Pt 2:9-10).

That messianic people has Christ for its head, "who was delivered up for our sins, and rose again for our justification" (Rm 4:25), and now, having won a name which is above all names, reigns in glory in heaven. The state of this people is that of the dignity and freedom of the sons of God, in whose hearts the Holy Spirit dwells as in his temple. Its law is the new commandment to love as Christ loved us (cf. Jn 13:34). Its end is the kingdom of God, which has been begun by God himself on earth, and which is to be further extended until it is brought to perfection by him at the end of time, when Christ our life (cf. Col 3:4) shall appear, and "creation itself will be delivered from its slavery to corruption into the freedom of the glory of the sons of God" (Rm 8:21). So it is that that messianic people, although it does not actually include all men, and at times may look like a small flock, is nonetheless a lasting and sure seed of unity, hope and salvation for the whole human race. Established by Christ as a communion of life, charity and truth, it is also used by him as an instrument for the redemption of all, and is sent forth into the whole world as the light of the world and the salt of the earth (cf. Mt 5:13-16).

Israel according to the flesh, which wandered as an exile in the desert, was already called the Church of God (2 Esdr 13:1; cf. Dt 23:1ff.; Nm 20:4). So likewise the new Israel, which while living in this present age goes in search of a future and abiding city (cf. Heb 13:14), is called the Church of Christ (cf. Mt 16:18). For he has bought it for himself with his blood (cf. Acts 20:28), has filled it with his Spirit and provided it with

19

January 12, 2009

Dear Holy Father,

Daily, I suffer a discomfort. I think it may be a guilty conscience. Fifty years ago, I would not have experienced this feeling. Although, I am sure I would or should have felt guilt for other sins and vices then. But, this ill feeling comes from my faith convictions that markedly differ from the teaching of my Roman Catholic Church and the opinions of my spiritual shepherds.

For years now, I have expressed my concerns to you on my conviction that the Church's Eucharist is not true to the teachings of Christ or to the covenant he performed for God, our Father. Recently, I find that the hypocrisy that Jesus characterized in his hierarchy (Mk 7:1–13) is in our hierarchy and is established in our Dogmatic Constitution on the Church (*Lumen Gentium*). This man-made law contradicts Christ's new and everlasting covenant (Jer 31:33–34) in order to cling to uncharitable traditions that purport to identify the Catholic Church with the Church of Christ. In truth and fact, I am convinced that the Church of Christ "subsists" in the Catholic Church (Ch. I, No. 8), but not when it is in Crusades, in Inquisitions, or in obedience to *Lumen Gentium*, Ch. II, No. 9. The Catholic Church has become a man-made and select community of believers in Christ—those baptized as Catholic. If Catholics do not save the rest of the people, the Church impliedly condemns them to a non-redemptive status or to perdition.

Plainly, *Lumen Gentium* is a contradiction between God and those select few spelled out above in Ch. II. It contradicts the earlier Ch. I defining of "The Mystery of the Church," which I discern to be all peoples making up humanity. See No. 8's description of the entity which Christ established as his holy church, as follows:

> This is the one Church of Christ which in the Creed
> is professed as one, holy, catholic and apostolic, which

our Savior, after his resurrection, commissioned Peter to shepherd (Jn 21:17), and him and the other apostles to extend and direct with authority (cf. Mt 28:18f.), which he erected for all ages as 'the pillar and mainstay of the truth' (1 Tm 3:15). This Church constituted and organized in the world as a society, *subsists* in the Catholic Church, which is governed by the Successor of Peter and by the bishops in communion with him, although many elements of sanctification and of truth are found outside of its visible structure. These elements, as gifts belonging to the Church of Christ, are forces impelling toward catholic unity. (Italics mine)

Vatican II tried to return the Catholic Church to this Church of Christ, but His Holiness Pope John XXIII died untimely. His successors promulgated and maintained a Dogmatic Constitution on the Church that clings to pre-Council teachings of uncharitable human tradition. As promulgated, *Lumen Gentium* disregards God's commandment of love in exchange for securing salvation for believers alone, a select community of the righteous—a community that condemns others to perdition. Before 1969, you taught that the Church was prevented from discriminating against "the many."

Since your doctoral dissertation, you have known that Christ's Church cannot be founded on the exclusion of anyone. The reason you may have been called is to sacrifice yourself as Jesus did for "the many."

Yours in Christ,

January 14, 2009

Dear Holy Father,

Let us view the Roman Catholic Church's version of *Lumen Gentium*, Ch. II, No. 9. It begins with an unloving claim that God created every man to be welcomed to God *if* he "fear him and does what is right." Peter is misinterpreted to have meant this when he spoke his words; "I begin to see how true it is that God shows no partiality" (Acts 10:34). However, our scribes ignore or misinterpret the passage, and they do show partiality when writing that God chooses only "a people." This allowed the scribes to claim that God prepared a select people "as a figure of that new and perfect covenant, which was to be ratified in Christ . . . ." It allowed the Church to redraft the covenant of Jer 31:31–34 and call only "those who believe in Christ" to be reborn in the Spirit as "a chosen race . . . ." This is not in the deal God made "on behalf of the many" (Mk 14:24). Christ extended the Covenant figure not to the few, but to all. His Cross redeemed the world.

Please, picture God deciding to create humanity, or picture Him intentionally creating humanity with free will to choose or not choose to love and do His will. In effect, they are created to sin, not as a purpose, but because God loves them as "good" whether sinning or not. According to you, God also decides that justice will be done by punishing some with eternal suffering. But, those who fear and do right by God, even loving out of fear, these few will be with God forever. This is the God that Catholics would portray to the world. This messianic people failed to redeem the rest of humanity for two millenniums by their portrayal of a God of justice and not love.

By our common knowledge, why are you not considering the version of a Loving God that Christ and my letters attempt to describe? We pose an ideal God of love, with whom Christ imprinted in us by our Catholic and Christian teachings on how to know God and His law of love. This view of all saved humanity sees "how true it is that God shows no partiality." Thus, God created man as sinners and saints to be loved and to try to love forever. Thus, from Christ's beginning, God pledged, and Christ teaches us how to know God and His law to

His satisfaction. Furthermore, God forgives our failures and remembers them no more, so God saves everyone.

With no strings attached, additional gifts were Christ's Eucharist, his story, and his presence to be impartially shared with all God's people and not just one Church or race. Thereby, God also teaches and receives love through Christ's story and intimate presence in each and every recipient. He does so in order to save "the many" (meaning "all" if charitably defined) and not just the few believers in Christ.

Common knowledge sees the Church of Christ as it "subsists" in the Catholic Church, but not while it excludes anyone, uncharitably or charitably, from its membership or Holy Communion. I will continue to try and spell out what Christ already imprinted in us. But, might I have a fatherly comment? It would sure help the morale of this writer.

Yours in Christ,

———————————————

January 16, 2009

Dear Holy Father,

I had hopes that the Holy Spirit called you to your present office because of your vast experiences that make you competent enough to steer our ship, the Church, back on course. For instance, you lived through Hitler's erroneous claims of a superior race, and you lived through the Holocaust, partially caused by Christendom's demeaning of the Jews. In Vatican II, called in part due to the Holocaust, you participated as an enthusiastic champion of the Church's new openness to non-Catholics. Later, you acknowledged our New Testament scholars' criticism of the exclusive Church's Eucharist, and as a product of Vatican II, you found "tempting" their contention that the Church's Eucharist should be unconditionally open to everyone, including non-Catholics (Ratzinger, *God Is Near Us*, p. 59).

Sadly, I now read an article in the Jesuit magazine *Popoli* (1/8/09) reporting that the Assembly of Italian rabbis felt that comments arguing the superiority of the Christian faith to be a proven fact and your decision to restore the Easter Week prayer for the conversion of Jews showed a lack of respect, canceling fifty years of ongoing interfaith dialogue and progress. I call that kind of disrespect bigotry. Another example of prejudice offending the faith convictions of other people was in your previous encounter with Islam's leadership, when you suggested they should be more reasonable in their principles and practice. These examples prove that you and the Catholic Church are too incompetent to redeem the world. The world needs Christ to perform the Covenant, and it needs Christ in Eucharist. It needs the Eucharist shared lovingly with everyone to continue God's teaching and forgiving of everyone created. He pledged to teach and forgive in Covenant, and Christ established it in performance.

You artfully set tradition over God's law when you delegated your responsibility concerning the exclusive Church's Eucharist to diocesan bishop's judgments in *Sacramentium Caritatis*. It reminds me of Pilate washing his hands of an issue which he well knew would be decided so adversely to Jesus. But, you can still correct the errors here by simply making the Church's Eucharist an inclusive Eucharist, working in Christ's way. Your apparent failure at dialogue with the rabbis and the Muslims proves the fallacy of *Lumen Gentium*'s messianic people's ability to redeem the rest of mankind. However, if tried, sharing the Eucharist sacrifice with everyone again allows the saving action of Christ that God obviously intended. Since creation's beginning, the Covenant's performance was to be God's alone. Jesus fatally committed himself to try God's way, and it resulted in God bringing good out of his glorious act of love.

Our failing efforts will also receive due recompense from Jesus Christ (2 Cor 5:10). You may be questioned on violating my vested rights in *Lumen Gentium*, for you are supposed to consider "with fatherly love the projects, suggestions and designs proposed by the laity." Also in No. 37, hope for a dialogue system for laity to communicate with our spiritual leaders is implied with this sentence, "In this way, the whole Church, strengthened by each one of its members, may more effectively fulfill its *mission for the life of the world*" (Italics mine). The hoped for dialogue has not familiarized. Has this wonderful hope of Vatican II died with Pope John XXIII? RSVP.

Yours open to dialogue,

_____

January 19, 2009

Dear Holy Father,

You argued the superiority of the Christian faith with the Jewish rabbis, and you contradicted the New Testament scholars in the superiority of your Bible translation over their expertise concerning the exclusive, rather than inclusive, Church's Eucharist (*God Is Near Us*, pp. 49–50). These, among other incidents, lead me to believe that even if you considered my letters, you long ago disdained the idea that Christ saves everyone regardless of the Catholic Church and its exclusive Sacrament. How can I ever carry a message of the Holy Spirit to you?

St. Augustine, your mentor, likely had conditioned you to his idea of us being conceived in original sin and not made superior by Christ's cross. You were raised to accept that the German people were superior, and you now are biased in feeling superior in faith to Jews, Muslims, and non-Catholics. Further armed with Holy Orders, you tend to assume that lay people have little to teach you, and if you assume that the Holy Spirit supports you with infallibility or such, what chance have my concerns to strengthen the Church by more effectively fulfilling its "mission for the life of the world?"

Your maintained *Lumen Gentium* professes that "God has given welcome to whoever fears him and does right" (Ch. II, No. 9). Apparently, you now conscientiously follow these opinions in directing a Church that selects a community of us who agree with you and excludes the mass majority of humanity from its body until we all agree to fear God and agree with what is right.

I cringe at Mass when I hear Father pray, "You were sent to heal the contrite . . . you came to call sinners" instead of the alternative Confiteor. The Eucharist sacrifice is the same event as Christ's sacrifice on Calvary. Christ saves the contrite, sinners, and all of us by his Cross and Covenant. I respectfully submit that your version of religion is not Christ's, and it denies the evidence of God's saving action to Jews, Muslims, New Testament scholars of Vatican II, and others who might reasonably dialogue on the issues.

Let Christ's Eucharist open up to everyone, and in time, Catholics' wrongdoings on earth will be erased. Meanwhile, your evildoing has already been forgiven. Except that Christ may chastise you when perfecting us all before we are all together as one Divinity.

Yours in Christ,

January 21, 2009

Dear Holy Father,

You seem to complicate what Christ simply established out of goodness and love for all humanity. Jesus Christ died to perform God's New and Everlasting Covenant (Jer 31:31 *ff*) and save everyone from everlasting death. Why can you not accept this plain reading of scripture, especially since you follow St. Augustine's rule to translate scripture in its most charitable interpretation?

Christ ratifies and performs God's pledge to forgive all evil on earth and His pledge to erase the memory of sin. Christ does this simply because God loves man as He created man, and man, with willingness to sin, naturally chooses evil in his self interest. So, Christ's Cross absorbs sins, cleansing mankind to meet God (Jer 31:31–34, 1 Cor 11:25, and Mk 14:24). Once saved, man may still be chastised.

God mandates that Christ is our only teacher, but you pride yourself on teaching Muslims and Jews that Christ has yet to save them. You teach in conformity to Church tradition that is not only contrary to Christ's demonstrative teaching, but is uncharitable to anyone but your people. It is understandable why your teaching that Muslims should be more reasonable offends Muslims, and it is understandable why your argument that your Christian ideas are better than Jewish religious ideas disturbs the rabbis. At Mass today, Hebrews 6:10–20 was read to tell us that Jesus anchored us to God's earlier covenant with Abraham, which equally benefits Muslims, Jews, and all co-inheritors of the same covenant. Still, Christ's blood of the New Covenant made Muslims, Jews, and all humanity coheirs better for salvation, without need of a messianic Catholic people to again redeem them or anyone else. God does it all, and Christ solely saves us regardless of what we do.

If I am wrong on reading Christ's new covenant and the effect of Jesus extending it to the whole of humanity, tell me where I err.

Yours in Christ,

January 23, 2009

Dear Holy Father,

God is Love. Yet, our Dogmatic Constitution On the Church (*Lumen Gentium*) opens Ch. II with, "At all times and in every race God has given welcome to whoever fears him and does what is right" (*cf.* Acts 10:35). From my earliest Catechism teachings I learned I am to know God, to love God, and to serve God as my main purpose in life. How accurately Jesus and Isaiah prophesied about hierarchies who pay lip service to Love, but with their hearts far from loving others, as they instead try to rule with fear. "Empty the reverence they do me because they teach as dogma mere human precepts" (Mk 7:6–8).

Besides erasing mention of God's goodness in forgiving all sins from our Church Constitution, which the appreciation of would put most of us at peace, the Catholic Church burdens us with a fear of God. According to the Church, we must do right in order to be acceptable to

Him. This fear of God's justice and fear of rejection by Him are means that religions use to control their members. It may fill pews, but Christ did not tell Peter to count his sheep. He told Peter to feed and care for them. Care connotes love, and sheep do better when left to browse by unfeared shepherds than when they are dogged into obeying.

True to the teaching of the Catholic Church, my pastor believes that Christ has not saved everyone. Retired Bishop Wiegand felt that I needed "obedience in faith" to the teaching of the Church concerning the the unworthiness in non-Catholics that exists despite Christ's blood redeeming the world. In regard to God's commandment of love, His Holiness Benedict XVI appears to be inconsistent between his writings and his actions after 1969. Around that time, he suffered a possible breakdown in relationships resulting in him changing universities and, perhaps, faith convictions. I suspect some unloving incident(s) occurred and hurt Father/Professor Joseph Ratzinger's feelings. I wait to be informed, corrected or reprimanded on my speculation. But, it seems that whatever occurred contributed to his ascension to his present position in our hierarchy, in spite of displaying enthusiasm to Vatican II openness.

Now that you represent Christ on earth, I urge you to open your heart again and at least respond to my suggestion or inquiries as Jesus Christ would do. Note that Jesus grieved when the Pharisees closed their minds and remained silent to his inquiries (Mk 3:1–6). As I believe Christ has already saved everyone for everlasting life, I try to enlighten you, not out of fear, but in thanks to Christ to prevent you and the Church from being a stumbling block to His continuing mission for the life of the world.

Yours in Christ,

_____

Dear Holy Father,

As you recall, His Holiness Pope John XXIII restrained the Curia to allow him and his assembled bishops to openly discuss and decide on matters of Vatican II. Still, the Curia participated and influenced the proceedings while Pope John lived. But on his death, the Curia was unrestrained and left to their devices, freely serving their own interests at the expense of those of us now regulated by *Lumen Gentium*. You witnessed what occurred, and you can correct my conjectures or remedy the wrongdoing that I see.

Previously along with Father Yves Congar, you showed public enthusiasm to the openness of Vatican II when the Council changed its interpretation from saying that the mystical body of Christ "is" the Catholic Church, to *Lumen Gentium*'s present reading that the Church of Christ "subsists" in the Catholic Church. You also showed enthusiasm to how it changed the passage that added "many elements of sanctification and of truth found outside of the visible structure. These elements as gifts belonging to the Church of Christ are forces impelling towards catholic unity" (Ch. I, No. 8). The Dogma's openness closes down later in Chapter II.

As Cardinal Joseph Ratzinger, you subsequently publicly argued a different opinion to the Chapter I Council's use of "subsists." Your argument changed it to mean that the Church of Christ "both is, and can only be <u>fully</u> present" in the Roman Church, with all its hierarchies. You also argued that Catholics faithful to the Church's teachings are the only ones worthy enough to participate in the Eucharist and the Church.

Surprisingly, when it came down to deciding the "central ritual" issue for an exclusive or an inclusive Eucharist, you delegated final judgment on the matter to diocesan bishops in *Sacramentum Caritatis*. In 1968, you found the ideas of the post-Vatican II scholars of the New Testament, those who criticized the exclusiveness of the Church's Eucharist, to be "tempting." They argued that it should be all-inclusive.

Still, you rejected their conclusions on questionable scriptural interpretations of your own, rather than tradition or the Church's teaching (*God Is Near Us*, pp. 59–60). I am at a loss to discern any rationale for your changing conviction, except that it may have to do with your ambitions to be Archbishop, Cardinal, and Pope. My suspicions also explain why you shied away from ruling on the central issue as you attained your goals. The Spirit may be in the "tempting" you felt and still feel. Or, maybe a more charitable reading of the Bible, which discerns that it does not contradict the New Testament scholar's idea (*Infra*, p. 59), may have weakened your rejection. The controversial issue remains yours to decide.

Open for discussion,

———————————————

January 28, 2009

Dear Holy Father,

Why am I out of step with you and the Roman Catholic Church? Fifteen years ago, when I was in-step, I was referred to an advanced study group of Catholics under our diocese's patronage, and I recall that a professor of theology from Loyola University taught us that one possessed of mortal sin should receive Holy Communion. I later read page 59 of *God Is Near Us*, where post-Vatican II scholars of the New Testament argued that Christ intended an open Eucharist, comparable to the Loyola theologian's opinion.

After three (3) years of learning about our post-Vatican II Church, I chose not to enter study for the Diaconate, but instead entered the Community of Passionist Partners (CPP). There, I recall strengthening in the belief that the crucifixion of Jesus was central to our faith, and Father Neil Parsons, CP, convinced me that Christ's Cross saved everyone. In heated discussions and from readings, such as *Lumen Gentium*, *God Is Near Us* (by Joseph Cardinal Ratzinger), etc., we discerned that marked differences in opinions existed among our spiritual leaders. Vatican II opened such disputes for controversy, like identifying the Catholic Church as the Church of Christ. By *ressourcement* to Christ in both Eucharist and Church, such identification would include every human being created, bar-none.

I learned from your writings, services, and lectures that the words of the Last Supper and the crucifixion of Jesus Christ instituted the central rite of Christ's Church and the Church itself. They were "interdependent," both Christ's words and death, and they saved us all by God's new covenant of Jer 31. However, the start of your inconsistencies appeared to me with your contention against the New Testament scholars, those who criticized the Church's Eucharist and contended it should be open to everyone with no strings attached. Accompanying your hierarchy elevations, other changes of opinion occurred, such as Jesus intending to found a particular church and the "for many" of Mark 14:24 would not prevent this church from selecting a few righteous members and condemning the rest to perdition.

Recently, an Associated Press article in my local paper awakened my hopes with reports of your inaugural YouTube. You welcomed the viewers by saying, "this great family that knows no borders." It thrilled me to read "this great family that knows no borders," because it fits Jesus' design of the Church of Christ, Vatican II's global church, and the mystical Spirit who "subsists" in the Catholic Church and in every individual human being. It is the people Christ recreated, and Vatican II acknowledged them as members of the Church of Christ.

The article also quotes Monsignor Claudia Maria Celli's statement that you are "a man of dialogue" who wants to engage with people wherever they are. I am here, willing to engage in any way you want, hoping Monsignor Celli is correct. *Lumen Gentium*, No. 37 points a way for us to go to be One.

Yours anxiously waiting,

January 30, 2009

Dear Holy Father,

The Museum of Jewish Heritage in New York is exhibiting creations by Father Patrick Debois' organization *Yahad in Unum* ("together" in Hebrew and Latin). The exhibit shows the Holocaust's extension into the Ukraine where Jews were methodically exterminated by bullets of Nazi mobile killing units at an estimated 82 people every hour. There are children too, stacked and shot in order.

Meanwhile, on the radio and published on the internet (NPR 1/26/09), you revoked the excommunications of four (4) Catholic bishops, including British Bishop Richard Williamson who upon hearing of his reinstatement, repeated on television his belief that evidence is lacking of "6 million Jews having been deliberately gassed in gas chambers as a deliberate policy of Adolph Hitler." Here the Catholic Church seems to deliberately widen the riff between it and Jews by concerning itself with internal Church relations at the expense of human credibility and God's law of love toward Jews.

As for excommunicating anyone, I do not believe the Spirit of Christ allows any excommunication. You should recall your doctoral dissertation, wherein St. Augustine remarked that the true Church could not subsist in the Donatists when they tried to deny their wayward priests the Sacrament. It removed the fundamental virtue of charity from Donatism, and therefore the true church could not subsist in Donatism. If Williamson is vincibly ignorant, you should publicly correct him, since he is your agent. But if he refuses to tell the truth, remove him as a Church authority and let the world know the extent of his ignorance. Plus, publicize his opinion as an anti-Christ attitude.

Meanwhile, simply obey Christ's order to "Take this and divide it among you" by interpreting the order in its more charitable translation. It should recognize that those ordered to receive are everyone whom Christ's death redeemed, which is every human being recreated as siblings by Christ and thusly constituting the mystical "body" of Christ (1 Cor 11:29). Thus, to avoid judgment on you, open the Church's

Eucharist to this "body" of Jesus Christ, and invite everybody. The post-Vatican II experts of the New Testament tried to enlighten us, but you traditionalists silenced them and negated God's commandment of love. You instead cling to human tradition where only Catholics are considered worthily clean (Mk 7:1–13).

For two millennia we have taught to love only those like us because we do not share our Church's Eucharist with everyone. Christ orders us to divide Eucharist with everyone, no strings attached, in order to experience today God's saving action in history. Instead, we are the "hypocrites" Jesus mentioned in Mark. We also are a Church at cross purposes to itself and to Christ, and we try to persuade even people of the book to love in ways other than God's design for us.

Yours in Christ,

_____

February 2, 2009

Dear Holy Father,

Bishop Jaime Soto, my diocesan spiritual leader, wrote about Eli to Samuel. He also wrote about John the Baptist to Andrew and another apostle. He wrote about them as exemplars of how we must share Christ so that others may come to recognize his true call echoing in minds and hearts. Christ Himself intended to be present when we invite them in Eucharist to "come and see."

In Jesus' redemption of mankind, God's pledge of imprinting the knowledge to know Him and His law of love in our hearts and minds is reinforced in every human during Holy Communion. The blood of the covenant fulfilled God's pledges of a future rebirth, which Jesus Christ fulfilled on the Cross. But, Jesus ordered a refresher meal for all of us because it was foreseen that happenings such as the Fourth Gospel, the Catholic Church, etc. would teach different from the notion that God/Christ alone performs the covenant of salvation.

Lumen Gentium, Ch. II, No. 9 contradicts the plan of God in favor of an uncharitable interpretation of scripture. Isaiah warned his troubled people about God's way, "For my thoughts are not your thoughts, nor are your ways my ways." Jesus quotes him elsewhere, "This people pays me lip service but their heart is far from me. Empty they do me because they teach as dogmas mere human precepts" (Mk 7:1–13). The Roman Catholic Church ignores these scripture passages and does it your way.

I again plead that you share Christ in Eucharist so that God may, as he intended, transform the faith and lives of all humanity Himself.

Yours anxiously waiting,

———————————————

February 4, 2009

Dear Holy Father,

I finished reading *American Lion*, by Jan Meacher, which is about the past USA president Andrew Jackson. He was a leader dedicated to freedom, but he failed to see liberty as a universal gift, as opposed to a particular gift for white nationalists. Instead of a lion, a political detractor characterized him as a fox in how he retained slavery of African-Americans and in how he destroyed and removed Native Americans from the USA to protect the status quo of his countrymen.

From the book, I see a parallel between Jackson and the Catholic Church. The Church should constantly broaden its love of humanity, but I find that its unloving Communion toward non-Catholics is Jacksonian in spirit. The Church must lovingly act toward the more enlightened collective reasoning of tomorrow. Also, in keeping with the Holy Spirit, we must be confident that the Church, while in error with its exclusiveness, will amend its wrongdoing by impartially exercising universal love, thusly preserving unity with Christ. Otherwise, the people of God will seek their own way for guidance by the Spirit, and they will set things right in Christ's way as to both Church and Eucharist.

Thus, you should wrest control of the universal Church of Christ— the global Church of Vatican II—from the traditionalists that Christ scorned (Mk 7:1–13).

Yours anxiously waiting,

February 6, 2009

Dear Holy Father,

I predict that the obvious and blatant error of the Roman Catholic Church's rejection of the truth—that Christ's spilled blood of the New Covenant saved every created human being—will be exposed as people become more enlightened. I believe you should correct the error soon to save face.

People openly consider the truth of Christ's words at the Last Supper and at every Eucharist sacrifice ". . . this is the cup of my blood, the blood of the new and everlasting covenant. It will be shed for you and for all . . . ." Those people will overcome the Catholics who have "obedience of faith" and blindly accept the teaching of the Church without question. *Lumen Gentium*'s unauthorized changes of the terms of the covenant, which negate the meaning of God's pledges of unilateral cleansing us of sin, will not be allowed to stand. The people of God of the "world church," the *Weltkirche* that Karl Rahner observed to emerge out of Vatican II, will reveal the truth—that the Church of Christ no longer "subsists" in the Catholic Church. We will return to the more charitable interpretation of the Bible, whereby the New Covenant (Jer 31) reads of God forgiving and forgetting all our evildoing. Thereby, we will have the "peace on earth" proclaimed by angels (Lk 2:14).

China, who now holds so much of the debts of the USA, may threaten to economically and socially dominate the world in the next half century. Yale Professor Lamir O. Sannah, a Catholic, wrote *Disciples of All Nations* and therein predicted that thirty percent of Chinese people will be Christians in the next century. They tend to anchor their thought and practice to their own cultural bonds. The Catholic Church faces troubled times, unless it returns to Christ's New Covenant (Jer 31) and lets Christ's way save humankind. God's favor rests on everyone through Jesus Christ, and "peace on earth" follows.

Vatican II marked the emergence of *Weltkirche*, or "world church," according to Karl Rahner's observation. Proof of this is in the statement in Ch. I of *Lumen Gentium* that says that the Church of Christ "subsists" in the Catholic Church, with forces outside of its visible structures impelling toward catholic unity (No. 8). I read you as an "ideologically partisan jurist" arguing against the Council's text (*The New Yorker*, 7/25/05), and I am confident that you can reverse your opinion to do it Christ's way.

My pleas to you may be moot, as it seems the Holy Spirit does it Christ's way regardless of interference by Catholics. I read scripture as meaning God's goodness alone saves everyone. We Catholics have yet to catch up with the true meaning of Christ's covenant. I remain concerned for our common good because you resist the call to love everyone, even though Christ's favor rests on each of us.

Yours in Christ,

_____

Dear Holy Father,

As an American, I learned that Vatican II made us both equal members of the Church of Christ, and I took this idea to heart. However, in my attempts to communicate with you, I discovered that the more important people in the Catholic Church do not act like I am of significance. You and your fellow clergymen behave as though you alone are the agents of the Church's mission. All of you neglect to "consider with fatherly love" my suggestions (*Lumen Gentium*, No. 37).

In the Dogmatic Constitution on the Church (*Lumen Gentium*), the liturgical assurances of Popes and assembled bishops spelled out that I had significance. Expressly, we laity were then vested with rights and obligations of a Constitutional nature. Being a citizen of the USA, I well appreciated these constitutional rights. Additionally, there were vested obligations placed on Catholics, among which was the obligation "to express their opinion on those things which concern the good of the Church" (*Lumen Gentium* Ch. IV, no. 37). In Christian obedience, I accepted these decisions of my assembled spiritual shepherds, and I attempted, through more than 200 letters, to follow the example of Christ in obedience to constituted authority. But, instead of receiving "fatherly advice" (also No. 37), I received silence and neglect, as though I am nothing. I am aware that humility calls for a nothing attitude, but Vatican II recognized me as a prophet, so I prophesize as if I am someone.

Initially, I expressed my critical opinion of the Church's exclusive Eucharist, and I urged in favor of the Eucharist of the post-Council scholars of the New Testament. You found their idea "tempting" at page 59 in your book, *God Is Near Us*. However, in struggling to communicate my concerns to you in various ways, my studies discovered the anti-Christ distortion of *Lumen Gentium* spelled out in Ch. II "On the People of God," which raised more concerns for the "good of the Church" that I am obligated to express to spiritual shepherds, whether or not they listen.

Christ died to perform God's New and Everlasting Covenant (Jer 31:31–34), but the Catholic Church changed the terms of this his last testament to claim that Christ redeems not all peoples, only those who "believe in Christ." Thereby, it follows that most of the world becomes excommunicated by Catholic fiat. The Church of Christ no longer "subsists," nor is in the Roman Catholic Church, so long as it persists in exclusion of our neighbors. God bounds us to love them as we love ourselves. Remember your doctoral dissertation on St. Augustine, wherein both of you concluded that the true Church could not be founded on the exclusion of others because it violates God's commandment of love.

Yours in Christ,

——————————————————

February 11, 2009

Dear Holy Father,

The reverse page concerns Jesus' Last Supper words from your book *God Is Near Us*. You write that Jesus' words reveal the significance of the Eucharist's institution in his anticipation of death where he shares Himself in body and blood to redeem the world. You emphasize that it is an act of self-sharing love offered to God and made available to mankind.

You point out that both the words and the death on the cross are "essentially interdependent," explaining that His death without His words would be a mere execution of Jesus for no discernible purpose. Although, not mentioned at page 29 (Infra) is the fact that the words of Jesus necessarily link His death to performing the New Covenant (Jer 31:31–34). You argued in your 1968/9 lectures on the Synoptics that the death "for many" (Mk 14:24) prevents the Catholic Church from becoming a select community and denying Christ's salvation to non-Catholics. Yet, at page 59 of your same book, you deny an open

Eucharist to those cleansed by Christ's Cross and God's Covenant as was espoused by our New Testament scholars.

From what has been imprinted in our informed consciences, you must be aware that Jesus Christ gave us the Eucharist as a memorial of His suffering and love. In worshipping His Sacrament, we are allowed by Christ to experience the salvation that He won for us, and experience the peace of the Kingdom that He introduced to us. I cannot understand how you can see Christ redeeming the world and still deny those in world salvation from His gift of love because they lack belief in God's Gift to them.

Knowing that God gifted me with eternal life through Jesus dispels the discrimination that I feel due to my spiritual leaders' treatment of my correspondences to you. Being a tool of the Holy Spirit has become a purpose-driven life. I am of significance in serving Christ and all mankind. Plainly put, I express my opinions on those things which concern the good of Christ's Church. I do so to reconcile the Catholic Church's Eucharist and Constitution to the Holy Spirit's control. Thereby, my contributions to correct the Church's wrongs may result in the production of the Spirit's fruits in Christ's way of love, joy, and peace for every human alive.

Yours in Christ,

_____

average sort of rabbi, such as might have lived in any age. Then it certainly does become incomprehensible for this rabbi suddenly to end up on the Cross, since people do not crucify the average professor. So it is not actually the real Jesus who breaks down on the Cross, but this notional Jesus does come to grief there. Seen from the viewpoint of the Cross, it becomes clear that Jesus was the kind of person who transcends all normal standards and who cannot be explained in normal terms. It would otherwise be incomprehensible for groups hostile to one another, Jews and Romans, believers and atheists, to join together to rid themselves of this remarkable prophet. He just did not fit into any of the ready-made categories people use, and therefore they had to clear him out of the way. There, again, it becomes clear that we cannot get to know the real Jesus by trimming him to fit our normal standards. Only the Jesus of the witnesses is the real Jesus. There is no better way of learning about him than to listen to the word of those who lived with him, who accompanied him along the paths of this earthly life.

If we question these witnesses, then we see—and this is in fact self-evident—that it was by no means a surprise to Jesus, something quite unforeseen, when he ended up on the Cross. He could hardly have been blind to the storm brewing up, to the force of the contradiction, enmity, and rejection that was gathering round him. It was of no less significance for his walking on toward the Cross with his eyes open that he lived from the heart of the faith of Israel, that he prayed the prayer of his people with them: the Psalms, which were inspired by the prophets and expressed the religion of Israel, are deeply marked by the figure of the righteous man who suffers, who for the sake of God can no longer find any place in this world, who for the sake of his faith endures suffering. Jesus appropriated this prayer, which we can see springing ever new, with ever deeper tones, both in the Psalms and in the prophets, from the Servant of Second Isaiah right up to Job and to the three young men in the fiery furnace; he made it intimately his own, filled it out, offered his own self for its sake, and thereby finally gave the key that opened up this prayer.[3]

Thus, in his preaching all paths lead into the mystery of him who proves the truth of his love and his message in suffering. The words he spoke at the Last Supper then represent the final shaping of this. They offer nothing entirely unexpected, but rather what has already been shaped and adumbrated in all these paths, and yet they reveal anew what was signified throughout: the institution of the Eucharist is an anticipation of his death; it is the undergoing of a spiritual death. For Jesus shares himself out, he shares himself as the one who has been split up and torn apart into body and blood. Thus, the *eucharistic words* of Jesus are the answer to Bultmann's question about how Jesus underwent his death; in these words he undergoes a spiritual death, or, to put it more accurately, *in these words Jesus transforms death into the spiritual act of affirmation, into the act of self-sharing love;* into the act of adoration, which is offered to God, then from God is made available to men. Both are essentially interdependent: the words at the Last Supper without the death would be, so to speak, an issue of unsecured currency; and again, the death without these words would be a mere execution without any discernible point to it. Yet the two together constitute this new event, in which the senselessness of death is given

---

[3] There is much valuable material on this in H. J. Kraus, *Psalmen*, vols. 1 and 2 (Neukirchen, 1960) [English trans. by H. C. Oswald, *Psalms 1–59* and *Psalms 60–150*, (Fortress Press, 1988–1989)]; and in H. U. von Balthasar, *Herrlichkeit*, vol. 3, pt. 2, *Alter Bund* (Einsiedeln, 1967) [English trans., *The Glory of the Lord*, vol. 6, *Theology: The Old Covenant*, trans. Brian McNeil and Erasmo Leiva-Merikakis (San Francisco: Ignatius Press, 1991)].

*Emphasis mine

February 13, 2009

Dear Holy Father,

You also were made for significance. Our Lord Almighty made us to please Him, and we live at three levels: (1) survival, (2) success, and (3) significance. Both you and I live at the success level and have learned that our mutual successes do not satisfy us in making a life for God.

You were made for far more than just succeeding to the Papacy, and you will never find significance in that position unless you learn to serve others by denying your life of possessions, pleasures, and positions. Significance comes from service—giving your life away for a purpose greater than yourself. According to Mark, Jesus said the following:

> If a man wishes to come after me, he must deny his very self, take up his cross, and follow in my steps. Whoever would preserve his life will lose it, but whoever loses his life for my sake and the gospel's will preserve it. What profit does a man show who gains the whole world and destroys himself in the process?

Try to fulfill the purpose that you were created for and that Christ called you for. You should know your reason for being Pope today is to lovingly serve God and all mankind. By inviting everyone to the Church's Eucharist and by accepting the fact that Christ's shed blood of the New Covenant saves every human being, you will step in Christ's footprints.

Some of this letter was plagiarized from the writings of Protestant Pastor and author Rick Warren's books *The Purpose of Christmas* and the *Purpose Driven Life*. Unfortunately, he too believes that to be saved one must believe in Christ. I am not saying that believers are not saved, but I emphatically contend that the New Covenant is a unilateral agreement by God to perform the entire deal. By his crucifixion and resurrection, Jesus extended the promised pledges to the Israelites to benefit all mankind.

Christ demonstrates the above lesson, and I literally accept it. I respectfully submit to you that Christ is our only teacher and that the New Covenant expressly rules out the need for any other one to teach us God's way and how to know the Lord (Jer 31:34).

Yours in Christ

———————————

February 16, 2009

Dear Holy Father,

In *Jesus of Nazareth*, you wrote, "Man knows himself only when he learns to understand himself in the light of God, and he knows others only when he sees the mystery of God in them." I assume that the mystery of God is in you, but I am still at a loss to know you. The fact that you are made in the image of God establishes that you are able to love everyone. And the fact that Christ's shedding of Covenantal blood has imprinted in you how to know God's law of love assures me that you know that you should share the Church's Eucharist with every human being. But, I do not see why you champion an exclusive Eucharist when Christ saves everyone, and God clearly said everyone is cleansed (Acts 10:28 and 11:18).

On pages 59 and 60 of *God Is Near Us*, you chose not to share the Church's Eucharist with the world because of your own personal translations of scripture from Jn 13:10, 1 Cor 11:27 *ff*, and a selection from Didache 10:6. You contradict the New Testament scholars' contention for a universal Eucharist. This is not the charitable translation of the Bible that your mentor St. Augustine taught you to use. It is more the wielding of proof texts of an "ideological partisan jurist" (*The New Yorker*, 7/25/2005, p. 43) who wants to reach some personal and uncharitable end. In the light of God and your non-response to my letters, your mindset remains a mystery.

On attaining your present Papal status, you washed your hands of the opportunity of significantly serving Christ's sanctification of us. In *Sacramentum Caritatis*, you artfully delegated the judgment of a universal Eucharist to be decided by conditioned diocesan bishops. Like Pilate, you knew the outcome as you left the real presence of Jesus to be uncharitably denied to nonbelievers and most of the world. God within you calls you to love us all.

Today, my Diocesan Statutes expressly state, "People who are not Catholic generally are not to receive Holy Communion." In "obedience of faith" to the teaching of the Church, our retired Bishop Wiegand negated the orders of Jesus Christ to take his Eucharist and "divide it among us" (Lk 22:17). Being a good servant of the Church, the bishop carried out your wishes to cling to man-made opinions and negate God's commandment of love, His covenant teaching, and His saving action in Christ. May the light of God show Most Reverend Bishop Soto that Christ is equally present in anyone alive, thanks to his redemption of us all.

Yours concerned,

February 18, 2009

Dear Holy Father,

On the reverse page, I copied a letter published in our Diocese newspaper. It mentions "Jesus' positive challenge to enjoy without guilt" the life everlasting that he bought for us. In his words and death, Jesus clearly demonstrated the performance of God's covenant pledges to teach and forgive us regardless of what anyone else teaches. In each of the Synoptic Gospels, we see spelled out the fact that Jesus saved the world by His shedding of His blood: "the blood of the *covenant*, to be poured out in behalf of many for the forgiveness of sins" (Mt 26:28), "the blood of the *covenant*, to be poured out on behalf of many" (Mk 14:24), and "[t]his cup is the *new covenant* in my blood, which will be shed for you" (Lk 22:20). I added the italicized emphasis. Also, the Covenant is Jer 31. for reference.

St. Paul agreed that Christ "died for all," so we no longer live for ourselves. We live for Jesus Christ, who died for us (2 Cor 5:15). Jesus Christ's same story is taught to people in the sacrifice of the Eucharist, which Paul received orders from the Lord to "do this in remembrance of me" (1 Cor 11:24–25). Paul also cautioned that if we do so "unworthily," we may bring judgment on ourselves. He qualifies his caution, "since it is the Lord who judges us, he chastens us to keep us from being condemned with the rest of the world" (verse 32). In view of God's Covenant pledges, I doubt if anyone will be condemned beyond Christ's chastisement, and since Jesus Christ will be judging us, I fully trust in his mercy. Anyway, excommunication is anti-Christ in spirit and fact, and thus, no divine authority exists to trump God's love.

I may have mentioned that Leonardo Da Vinci drew a sketch of the Apostle John asleep at the table when Da Vinci prepared his painting of the Last Supper. One of London's museums possesses the sketch. If John wrote the Fourth Gospel, the sketch explains why he makes no mention of the Synoptics' words instituting the Eucharist—the same words you explained were "essentially interdependent" with Jesus' death and "without these words would be a mere execution without any discernible point to it" (*God Is Near Us*, p. 29). Much of John's Gospel is man-made opinion that negates Christ's last words. John admits Christ spoke his words as God instructed (Jn 12:49–50) but omits too much.

We should enjoy the gift of Christ without guilt because His Covenant does not depend on a requisite "to believe" (John 8:24). Christ forgives our evildoing and remembers our sins no more (Jer 31:34) solely by His universal performance of the covenant. He thereby saves us without faith or works.

However, John's Gospel and the Catholic Church insist only those "who believe in Christ are reborn" (*Lumen Gentium*, Ch. II, No. 9). Yet, God's covenant and Jesus' dying words save us all by Divine power alone. Who teaches you—Christ or the Catholic Church's traditionalists?

Yours concerned,

_____

Have joy without guilt

F ather Ron Rolheiser wrote in the Commentary section (The Herald, Jan. 24) about "celebrating." I enjoyed the commentary, especially his view of today: "We tend to read the Gospels selectively so as to ignore Jesus' positive challenge to enjoy without guilt."

This is so true at Mass, where we hear again and again Jesus saying his shed blood is of the new and everlasting covenant. Yet we do not know the terms of God's deal. We should study that covenant (see Jeremiah at 31:31ff) to appreciate that God, through Christ, saves every human sinner from everlasting death. We should have joy without guilt because Jesus Christ unilaterally does it all for everyone in bearing all sins out of love for us.

Since the Mass celebrates Calvary's self-same sacrifice, to which we witness at the foot of the cross as time and space are arrested, we should celebrate with joy and thanksgiving Jesus' covenantal gains for us. By having Christ's actual presence intimately within us at Communion, we are assured that we are loved as we are and may depart Mass transformed to lovingly share ourselves with the world as Christ intended.

Fred Ithurburn, Yuba City

February 23, 2009

Dear Holy Father,

I struggle to understand the essence of the Paschal mystery. I understand some saints grasped it and shared in the life of Christ by dying with him. It reminds me of a movie, *Sophie Sholl: The Final Days*, which I saw the end of. The title character was a student who in 1943 participated in distributing pamphlets telling the German people of their nation's Holocaust and the need to stop the bloodshed. The guillotine summarily executed her for harming Hitler's war efforts. Sophie was a contemporary of yours who served her country. Her priest confirmed that, like Christ, she gave up her life to save her people from repercussions in prolonging the dirty war.

In 1943, you supported your fuehrer with the faith that most of your countrymen blindly gave him. He persuaded you to believe that you were, by nature, a special race and had a mission to faithfully follow him. Today your allegiance is to the cause of the Catholic Church and as its spiritual leader to supporting the Dogmatic Constitution on the Church (*Lumen Gentium*) and its mission to unite the whole human race to its way of belief. In Friday's reading of Genesis 11:2 *ff*, a parallel came to me where people built a community edifice based on their mutual understanding, seeking to make significance for themselves. Plainly, the Church alters God's New Covenant and attempts to seize Christ's authority and usurp Christ as the redeemer of the World, for its own significance.

Hitler and Babel differ from the Catholic Church in how the latter's authority is supposedly from God, and its purpose is to be charitably responsible for everyone in the world. Thus, the Church of Christ "subsists" in the Catholic Church (*Lumen Gentium* Ch. I, No. 8). However, the Catholic Church is not identified with the Church of Christ so long as it excludes anyone from its sacraments, especially

Christ's universal Eucharist. The Catholic Church is not being charitably responsible for everyone's redemption as Christ is.

Unlike Fuehrer Hitler's master race or Babel's people, the people of God whom you represent are all humanity. By the light of God's law of love within you, you can see that we all equally have the mystical Body in us. But, that is not what Catholics built in their Dogmatic Constitution on the Church (*Lumen Gentium* Ch. II, No. 9), in which the opening paragraph contains what Jesus prophesied as hypocrisy occurring (Mk 7:6–8). By deleting essential terms of God's covenant pledge and deforming the last testament of Jesus Christ, the Church erects a tower of Babel. Thereby, it synthesizes an anti-Christ precept to adopt the Fourth Gospel's redemption only "for those who believe in Christ," rather than the Synoptic's view that Christ's blood of the New Covenant saves all humanity regardless of our worthiness. Catholic believers save themselves and become a messianic Christian people to redeem the rest of mankind. You pay Our Lord "lip service" and do not accept that Christ alone saves us simply out of the goodness of God.

Please take a lesson from Sophie and establish Christ's truth that saves all people and favors none. I again suggest you do it Christ's way with an Easter Mass invitation to the entire world to consume the Lord's Supper and allow Christ to build his Kingdom with everyone united in His love.

Yours in Christ,

Dear Holy Father,

Earlier, I informed you that I was a lay partner with the Passionist Fathers. As you know, St. Paul of the Cross founded the Congregation from the 1750s until his death in 1775. He too wrote letters, and they were published in three volumes. Paul spent his life evangelizing, centered on the cross and the Passion of Jesus "in view of the emergence of de-christianization that already existed but was not seen" (Introduction to Volume Three, by Adolfo Lippi, C. P., page xiii).

A major influence on my thinking has been meditation on the Passion of Christ, struggling to know the profound mystery of God in the saving action of Jesus Christ. St. Paul of the Cross prayed in thanksgiving for Christ's drawing of us all onto the Cross in his prayerful offerings to God. In my studies too, I thank your contribution of God Is Near Us for enlightening me on the fact that the Synoptic's words of the Last Supper, instituting Church and Eucharist, are "interdependent" with the death of Jesus, thus explaining the mystery as more than a mere execution. But, Catholics do not place the words and death in context of the New Covenant and, in effect, abandon a faith centered on the cross that concerned Paul T.

Also like Paul of the Cross (Paul T), I try to bring to light my concern for the good of the Catholic Church in its "de-christianization," which has existed for centuries based on human traditions that disregard God's commandment of love, excommunicating most of God's people and excluding from redemption all but "those who believe in Christ," (Lumen Gentium, Ch. II, No. 9). I respectfully suggest that the Fourth Gospel is the contributing cause to our anti-Christ ignoring of the Cross and Covenant.

An advertisement in my current NCR (2/20/09) stating the opinion of Rev. Donald Senior, C.P., that John's Gospel is just as authentically "historical" as the Gospels of the Synoptics disappoints me. Note Father Senior has been an addressee of copies of my letters to you. He never responded to any. I have a copy of his book on John's version of the Passion, and I suspect more of the same opinions are in what he is selling. He does not rebut my opinions of the Fourth Gospel and its impact on our "de-christianization." Christ and the New Covenant need no teachings to improve on how to know His Redemption and God's pledges of forgiving and teaching everyone to Our Lord's satisfaction. In Mass, Christ's story imprints in our hearts, especially with receipt of Holy Communion, the fact God loves us and, solely through Divine goodness, teaches us to know the Lord. The "de-christianization" of the Eucharist substitutes the Roman Catholic Church for Jesus Christ's role as savior and teacher.

Open for discussion,

_____

February 27, 2009

Dear Holy Father,

The Fourth Gospel does not evidence the history of God's saving covenantal action. Actually, John's Gospel, for all of the author's faith, may blaspheme against the Spirit. My bible's footnote No. 12, 31*f* of Mathew's Gospel describes a blasphemy of the Pharisees denying the presence of God in Jesus because "it negates the evidence of God's saving action in history." Anyone who denies that God unilaterally saves everyone through Christ's efforts might commit the unforgivable blasphemy against the Holy Spirit. Thus, I believe our faith, good works, and evildoing have no effect on our salvation and will be considered only in chastisement.

The Fourth Gospel may salvage God's saving action in respect to the Eucharist in John's "Discourse on the Bread of Life" (Jn 6:25–70). But, my bible also footnotes that most scholars today think of the bread in these verses as primarily a figurative reference to Jesus' revelation or teaching. However, there may be a secondary reference to the Eucharist in verses 51–58 where the Eucharistic theme comes to fore. Verse 51's last two lines are noted in comparison to Luke's words, "This [bread] is my body which is given for you" (Lk 22:9). Also, verses 54–58 use the verb "feeds" to mean "munch or gnaw" and may be the author's emphasis on real flesh and blood of Jesus (Jn 6:55) to personify the Bread of Life.

Still, the authors of the Fourth Gospel had access to the Synoptic's version of Jesus' words at the Last Supper, which Mathew, Mark, and Luke each mentioned how Christ's sacrificial redemption of all human beings is made in the context of the New Covenant (Jer 31*ff*). But, neither the Fourth Gospel nor the Dogmatic Constitution on the Church (Lumen Gentium), promulgated by Pope Paul VI on November 21, 1964, are true to Jesus' parting words, words which evidence God's saving action in history. God meant Christ's "blood of the new and everlasting covenant" to be shed from creation's beginning for everybody, and that is the mystery of faith memorialized in Eucharistic Prayers at Mass. Father Senior C.P.'s characterization of John's Gospel as a "style of Jewish literature" further distances us from the truth of Christ's New Covenant way of redemption. Also, his championing of Jesus' origin as the Word of God in "poetic" prologue overlooks the more likely scholarship that the Prologue's "Logos" is from the Stoic school and supports the Hellenistic religious influence on Ephesians where gods fathered children with earth mothers, to explain the Son of God. A contradiction is implied in the Prologue—any who do not accept him as God are not empowered to become children of God (Jn 1:12), but God still begets us by willing, not man willing to believe (Jn 13).

Yours open to dialogue,

———————————————

March 2, 2009

Dear Holy Father,

Human traditions are taught as dogmas once they take hold as habits. My past Pastor Joe Bishop contended that holding hands at Mass during the Our Father took away from the Sign of Peace. But today in my parish, most of the congregation holds hands with the presider before the Sign of Peace.

Recently, a new behavior is occurring at the end of Mass. Our presiders have the Body of Christ displayed outside of the tabernacle for adoration. It disturbs my Eucharistic prayers because at the same time I am trying to interiorly focus on Our Lord's actual presence to leave the Church transformed, I leave the Church disregarding the obviously exposed body of Christ. I think, as did Father Bishop, that the sentimental ritual takes away from Christ's purpose for the Eucharist. The ritual concerns me because it may become part of Mass.

Empty is the reverence the Church does Christ when it teaches us dogmas of uncharitable human precepts (Mk 7:1–13). Disregarding God's law of loving everyone created as equals and worthy to receive Holy Communion, the Church Eucharist evidences the power that unauthorized tradition becomes. In your edited sermon at pages 59 and 60 of God Is Near Us, you cite mere human precepts of John's Gospel, Corinthians, and Didache to support your uncharitable opinion contradicting the post-Vatican II experts on the New Testament who championed an open Eucharist for everyone. Sadly, you and my spiritual leaders seem unanimous in disregarding the covenant of Jesus Christ, "This cup is the new covenant in my blood. Do this whenever you drink it, in remembrance of me" (1 Cor 11:25). The tradition you respect makes unworthy those that the covenant made worthy of Christ.

The New and Everlasting Covenant is that of Jer 31:31 *ff*, 1 Cor 11:25, Mt 26:28, Mk 14:24, Lk 20:22, and every Eucharistic Prayer's invocation of the Holy Spirit. Thus, Christ is our teacher and savior, not the Catholic Church in its traditions. Let us return to the Church of Christ which "subsists" in the Catholic Church unless the latter ceases excluding others unlovingly. Christ gave us a gift with no strings attached, but we ungraciously rejected it and made up our own Eucharist and our own Redemption by tradition instead.

Open for Discussion,

_____

March 4, 2009

Dear Holy Father,

I suggest that God's saving action in the history of Christ performing the New Covenant is not evidenced in the Fourth Gospel. Although I suspect Mathew's Gospel took liberties too, e.g., the family trip to Egypt is inconsistent with the other gospel's time and space; but, his passage on the blasphemy against the Spirit may be inspired. My bible's footnote No. 12, 31 *ff* (Infra) mentions denial of the presence of God in Jesus "negates the evidence of God's saving action in history." So, too, does the Fourth Gospel's omission of Christ's words of fulfilling the New Covenant by his sacrificial death on the Cross; and, requiring belief teaches an anti-Christ way.

"John's Gospel" may salvage the Eucharist memorial being included in John's "Discourse on the Bread of Life" (Jn 6:25–70); but, my bible also footnotes that most scholars today think of the bread in these verses as primarily a figurative reference to Jesus' revelation or teaching . There may be a secondary reference to the Eucharist; however, in verses 51–58 where the Eucharist theme comes to fore. Verse 51's last two lines are 54–58 use the verb "feeds" to mean "munch or gnaw" and may be the author(s)' emphasis on real flesh and blood of Jesus (Jn 6:55). Also, the discourse may be a later add on as is its appendix.

Still, the author(s) of John's Gospel had access to the Synoptics' version of Jesus' Last Supper words in the context of Paul's church in Ephesus from where he wrote to Corinth what "I received from the Lord . . . This cup is the new covenant in my blood." (Emphasis mine). Paul spoke the words of the Glorified Christ, repeating his Last Supper words, which you appreciate are "interdependent" (God Is Near Us, page 29) with Christ's death that redeemed mankind, making those words central to Christianity. Unfortunately, you and the Catholic hierarchy have aggrandized John's Gospel and its "historical authenticity" to negate the evidence of God's saving action in covenant and in Christ's unilateral performance of God's covenant. Your way may be anti-Christ.

Can you not see that the Logos of John's Prologue is of the Stoic school and is based on the Helenists at Ephesus teaching gods fathering children with earth mothers. The belief in Christ becomes a duty essential for "obedience of faith" in Church teaching (see Bishop Wiegand's 7/14/07 letter).

Open for discussion

March 6, 2009

Dear Holy Father,

The advertisement in NCR (2/20/09) worries me. Father Donald Senior, C.P. claims that the Fourth Gospel, which has no mention of God's New Covenant, is as authentically historical as the Synoptic's version of the Last Supper.

Your teaching and/or preaching that the Last Supper words of Jesus are "interdependent" with his death (God Is Near Us, p. 29), when combined with the New Testament scholars' common acceptance that the scriptural accounts of Jesus' passion and death are closer to history than any other part of the Gospel, tends to make the Synoptics' last words historical narrative, even as stylized text of biased witnesses. St. Paul wrote that he "received from the Lord" (1 Cor 11:23) and quoted the glorified Jesus saying, "This cup is the new covenant in my blood." Adding his version belies the authenticity of John's Gospel being as authentically historical as the Synoptic's. The foot washing is nothing compared to the Lord's words at Supper.

However, Pope Paul VI and the curia he released from the restraints of Pope John XXIII promulgated the <u>Dogmatic Constitution on the Church</u> and therein erased God's New Covenant pledges, nullifying Christ's unilateral performance of the Covenant in his death and his Eucharist. We artfully made our own words to redeem believers as the "many" (<u>Mk</u> 14:24), condemning all others to perdition.

I trust that God, through Christ, saves everyone by our Lord's unilateral performance of the new covenant. The Catholic Church's interpretation of the mystery of Christ and Father Senior's C.V.s teach mere human precepts as dogma, nullifying God's law of love. Instead, we love non-believers less than we love believers.

Open for correction,

_____

March 9, 2009

Dear Holy Father,

Have you asked your self why the pledges of God are removed in our Dogmatic Constitution from the new covenant version of the Bible? The curia had been reinstated to power at the time of the dogmas promulgation and their fruits are obvious. Why maintain them?

Constitutions, as in the USA, are made partly in defense of government against citizens. U.S.'s freedom from a monarchy raised the Whiskey Rebellion, when we taxed our rebellious citizens. The Roman Catholic Church hierarchy has defended its turf for centuries. Placing popes and magisteruims superior to Christ's covenantal authority is the curia's defensive measure. <u>Lumen Gentium</u> concededly avoids the word "monarchy" and even allows that the laity "cannot err in matters of faith" if they are in unanimity with the bishops, but the twists the Curia adds to the new covenant places the Church over Christ being savior and teacher. Our Lord's forgiving humans is replaced by Church's sacraments redeeming Catholics. The curia's paranoia is relieved by making sure the Church is essential for redemption.

The fear of an already redeemed and knowledged humanity, threatening the hierarchy's job may be why the Dogmatic Constitution 's distortion of the covenant appears. Christ's order to repeat his Lord's Supper, if practiced correctly, will keep our clergy busy in service throughout the world until the ends of time. Our Eucharistic Prayers preserving Christ's ideal, should be proclaimed by our clergy, in Eucharistic sacrifices everywhere to everyone.

I am convinced, whether or not you have read any of over two hundred (200) letters to you, that you know of what I write and the letters will refresh your memory if the curia allow you to read them, or correctly summarize the points of concern for your recollection. I doubt the curia will help if your more advanced years have taken a toll on your memory. Also, a loss in control of the curia may be evidenced when they recently led you to reinstate the obtuse bishop who denies the holocaust. Your interests may not coincide with that of the curia in knowing what is good for you to know.

In any case, I pray that the Holy Spirit aid us to reinstate Christ as Our Lord over and above the Roman Catholic Church's self interests.

Hopefully yours,

_____

March 11, 2009

Dear Holy Father,

In 1966, you published a book, <u>Theological Highlights of Vatican II</u>, where you enthusiastically wrote of the Church's new openness and wholeheartedly affirmed the council. The Second Vatican Council was held from 1962 until 1965 and greatly influenced by Pope John XXIII, until he died in 1963. Pope Paul VI then dropped the issue of reforming the curia and returned it to favor in time to promulgate the <u>Dogmatic Constitution on the Church</u>.

You were there and experienced that Pope John and his assembled bishops were actually working as servants of servants in trying to connect us back to Christ at the Last Supper. The council freely attempted to develop ressourcement and correct past errors in interpreting Christ's way. It even reached out to people like me to travel the road of learning and professing. Pope John secured us in faith to accept that "Christ is ever resplendent as the center of history and of life," but only while he lived as Vicar. By 1968, you became a protagonist to restrict the Council's openness and Pope John's impact.

The above thoughts were drawn from my reading of journalist John Wilkin (<u>Commonweal</u>, 2/27/09). Apparently, changes in the Church since Vatican II disturb Wilkin. He claims to be a witness and a child of Vatican II. He became a Catholic by desire on witnessing his first Roman Catholic Mass. There, unlike his Anglican Eucharist, the whole congregation went to receive Holy Communion. "This is the real thing," he thought. The curia's leading of you to restate Bishop R. Williamson has disillusioned Wilkin into falling back on "conscience is the aboriginal Vicar of Christ" to stay, with Cardinal Newman, as Catholic. I suggest that Christ and conscience suffice until the Church repents.

From the beginning, the Council's openness perturbed Pope John Paul II, then Archbishop Karol Wojtyla, because in Poland the episcopate's discussions were in secret to maintain unity in the Church. However, whatever changed you between the publication in 1966 and your contradiction of the New Testament scholars' contention for an open Eucharist (<u>God Is Near Us</u>, pages 59 and 60) leaves me hope to your reawakening to Christ's Spirit and his way of charity being the only way to follow Christ.

I note the <u>Commonweal</u> edition reports that <u>Didache</u> was written in Syria between 160 and 180 A.D. Also, <u>Didache</u> competes with the verb <u>eucharistein</u>, "to give thanks," as found in 1 <u>Cor</u> 11:23–25 in being early reference of the Lord's Supper as "the Eucharist." In <u>God Is Near Us</u> you cite both writings to support your opinion. I invite you, in the interest of openness and the Church's Eucharist, to re-discern St. Paul's verse 25 with an open heart and accept that Paul "received from the Lord" the new covenant remembrance. <u>Didache</u> was man-made, but Christ speaks his words, "interdependent" with his sacrifices on Calvary and at Mass, as the Lord God instructs Him to speak. Thus, the Covenant establishes our relationship with God and not the Dogmatic Constitution on the Church.

Yours in Christ,

_____

March 13, 2009

Dear Holy Father,

In reading an article published in <u>NCR</u> (3/16/09), it dawned on me that former British Prime Minister Tony Blair admirably steps in the footsteps of Jesus Christ to counter extremism within respective creeds in order to enhance global security and harmony. He offers a course on the topic, in his Faith Foundation at Yale University, and makes the course enrollment available elsewhere.

Tony Blair states that he was influenced to become a Christian by assurances that his concern for the welfare of his militantly atheistic father should be dispelled because God loves us in spite of our evildoing. God needs no love in return to forgive us. Since then, he converted to his wife's Catholic faith, and Hans Küng's Global Ethics Foundation has influenced him. Blair argues that there are global solutions which are more important than us and "there are limits to humanism and beyond; those limits, God, and only God, can work."

In contrast, our <u>Dogmatic Constitution on the Church</u> attempts to change God's relationship with humankind by distorting the New Covenant (<u>Jer</u> 31:31–34). It negates proof of God's work having already forgiven the evildoing of all people. Therein, we claim that Christ's New Covenant, instituted in His Blood, redeems only "those who believe in Christ," and we claim favor as the redeemed "messianic people" who are delegated the work of Christ to redeem the rest of the world. However, as <u>Lumen Gentium</u> Ch. II, No. 9 is promulgated by Pope Paul VI and his curia; it negates the global church of Christ that Pope John XXIII and his assembled bishops deem, infallibly, to "subsist" in the Catholic Church (Ch. I, No. 8). Jesus told us, "the kingdom of God will be taken away from you and given to a people yielding its fruits." I would think that Pope John, Hans Küng, Tony Blair, etc. are such people in whom the Church of Christ "subsists," and someday may be given the kingdom, if you don't awaken.

Yours in Christ,

———————————————

March 16, 2009

Dear Holy Father,

Last Friday's letter on the Tony Blair article in <u>NCR</u> (3/6/09) contained an interesting item on our President Barack Obama, who was at the same annual prayer breakfast in D.C. when Blair related his inspiration of the "unconditional nature of God's love. A promise perpetually kept. A <u>covenant</u> never broken" (Emphasis mine).

President Obama also related how the example of faith-filled community organizers out of a Catholic Church on Chicago's South Side had led him to become a Christian. The Spirit of Christ works in myriad ways, and perhaps what worked on Obama were those believers in Christ who had "obedience of faith" to the teaching of the Church (Lumen Gentium, Ch. II, No. 9) and worked as the "messianic people" to redeem the world. I just speculate on the faith the organizers follow.

I still favor obedience of faith in Christ and God's pledge in "a covenant never broken," doing the work that "only God can work" in imprinting in Obama's mind and heart how to know God and God's law of love. Of course, like Blair, I wish not to diminish the work of humanists who give themselves for others, but there are limits to what humanism can do, and I credit the Holy Spirit with teaching all of us.

Placing salvation or redemption in the hands of the Catholic Church—as Lumen Gentium, Ch. II, No. 9 purports to do by changing the words of the New Covenant (Jer 31:31–34) to redeem "those who believe in Christ," assigning to the redeemed the task of saving the rest of the unredeemed—borders on blaspheming the Holy Spirit (footnote 12, 31 *f* of the Gospel According to Matthew). I trust that the earlier Ch. I, No. 8 truth, that the Church of Christ "subsists" in the Catholic Church, takes precedence over the later anti-Christ work, and we can still amend our way to that of Christ's way of the true New Covenant.

I submit that God unilaterally performs the New Covenant in Christ's blood as it is the work that only God can work effectively. Therein, Christ redeems the world and leaves us the global Church of Christ, whose membership includes all humanity. It subsists in the Catholic Church when the latter acknowledges that Christ alone is our teacher and savior, as scripture establishes.

Open for argument,

March 18, 2009

Dear Holy Father,

To this point I hope that you read some of my letters because I believe you previously entertained the same thoughts. But I have come to think that I am dealing with a very bizarre psyche that exists in the permanent bureaucracy of the Vatican. It is to its interest to be detached from reality and cling to the fantasy of tradition. Their leading of you into reinstating Bishop Williamson, an error that you recently acknowledged, evidences their control. The news adds to my conviction that no group of moral men is infallible.

I think that Vatican II's constitutional obligation caused me to be "obligated to express my opinion" on things I truthfully believed concern the good of the Church (No. 37, <u>Lumen Gentium</u>). It concedes that we have the vested right to criticize and correct the wayward course of the Church. Thus, when it is obvious to me that Jesus Christ died to establish God's New Covenant for the eternal life of the world (<u>Jer</u> 31:31–34 and 1 <u>Cor</u> 11:25, <u>Mk</u> 14:24, etc.) and the post-Vatican II theologians and New Testament scholars' sensibly contend that Christ meant for the Eucharist to be unconditionally open to everyone, excommunicating anyone becomes a contradiction of God's saving action and a blasphemy against the Holy Spirit. Consequently, I become acutely bound to pursue God's saving action in history, and I publicly reveal the anti-Christ in the distortion of the New Covenant (No. 9, <u>Infra</u>) that has been present ever since the deletion of God's forgiveness has allowed the myth of unworthy communicants.

Scripture advises us to point out fraternal corrections, and if we are not listened to or if we are ignored, "refer it to the Church" (<u>Mk</u> 18:17). I refer this concern to the Church of Christ that, most times, subsists in the Catholic Church, as most of Christ's Church's members are denied His Eucharist. In my occupation, the usual means of complaining to everyone about denied rights is to file a lawsuit and litigate this issue to a jury. Litigation against the Catholic Church, whose corporate body extends into California, may be in any court of general jurisdiction, and we can try the case in Sacramento. However, a heartfelt restraint holds me from subjecting my Church to the huge monetary verdict that a local jury would likely award.

I can limit it and sue for the breach of the part of our Dogmatic Constitution's implied representations, upon which I relied, that if I corresponded, my spiritual shepherds would respond (Lumen Gentium, No. 37), rather than ask a jury to award reasonable damages commensurate with the value of the Eucharist they were denied, as evidenced in the Diocesan Statutes of the Third Diocesan Synod. In asking for my out-of-pocket loss, I can still tell the story of Lumen Gentium, No. 9's perfidy and the Church's lack of love of neighbor in its Eucharist practice.

What do you suggest I do?

Sincerely yours,

———————————————

March 20, 2009

Dear Holy Father,

I seethe each time I consider the misquoting of the New Covenant (Jer 31:31–34) in our Dogmatic Constitution on the Church. His Holiness Pope Paul VI promulgated it, so I presume the curia inscribed it as distorted in No. 9, Chapt II of Lumen Gentium to misenlighten nations. Thus, The Roman Catholic Church teaches mere human precepts as dogmas in negation of God's saving action and Christ's redemption of the world. Instead, clinging to Church tradition, we are taught a human way of salvation wherein "those who believe in Christ" are reborn alone as the messianic people. Christ will use a "small flock" to redeem the rest of humanity, presumably because Christ is inept.

Typescripts of your lecture notes on theology from 1968/9 taught that Jesus' words at the Last Supper founded the Church. He linked the new covenant (Jer 31) to the "for many" (Mk 14:24), thusly preventing the Church from becoming a select community of the righteous, which would condemn everyone else to perdition (see <u>Commonweal</u>, 4/21/08). Also, you preached that these same <u>eucharistic words</u> transform Jesus' death into an act of self-sharing love, interdependent with his death, and an offering to God, who makes it available to us all (<u>God Is Near Us</u>, page 29). Thus, Jesus' words and death together constitute the performance of the New Covenant relationship, making everyone "worthy" to receive the Eucharist and be the sibling of Christ, simply by God's goodness and Christ's perfect performance. Plainly, it is a unilateral divine Covenant not to be bilaterally performed by God and man.

Perhaps it is too much to ask His Holiness Pope Benedict XVI to exercise the courage of his convictions and put to rest the human precepts that serve as base for the Church's exclusive Eucharist and Dogmatic Constitution. An improvement just as you corrected the error of restating Bishop Williamson and courageously informed us that the curia made you do it. Or just act simply as Jesus did when he ate with the unwashed people and disregarded the complaints of his hierarchy's traditions in order to obey God's commandment of love (see <u>Mk</u> 7:1–13).

Our Catholic Church is assigning the entire works of Jesus, at the Last Supper and on the Cross, to the principles of human precepts expressed as dogma in <u>Lumen Gentium</u>. It is anti-Christ because it denies us the lesson of Christ's saving action in the New Covenant. Can't you see this, or is your expertise too focused on opinions regarding AIDs, contraceptives, and such?

Open for fatherly discussion,

_____

Dear Holy Father,

I am informing you of my intent to sue our Church in hopes you will dissuade me. I think I am not harsh in light of Jesus prophesizing against the "hypocrites of his hierarchy who clinged to human tradition and nullified God's word (Mk 7:1–13). Also, when he died as a criminal on the cross to institute the New Covenant (Jer 31–34) which our present hierarchy fraudulently distorts (Lumen Gentium, Chapt II, No. 9) for its own self-interests and deceitfully negates God's saving relationship with all of us, in the circumstances I feel duty bound to proceed.

In the US we are free to criticize our government. As the people of the Church of Christ we have an obligation to speak truth to power. A church in which members cannot criticize its policies is a church without the means of correcting its wayward course. Lumen Gentium, No. 37, thus, obligates us to express "opinion on those things which concern the good of the Church" to fulfill its mission to humanity. This I am trying to do.

My primary concern is the exclusive Church's Eucharist which denies Catholicism from being true to the Church of Christ because of uncharity in exclusion of anyone from its Sacrament. In attempting to express this concern, I discovered an even clearer evidence against God's law of love. It is in the Church purporting to quote truth about the past, and to correctly quote a past document is an essential rule. Our Dogmatic Constitution, as constrains those who govern from distorting agreements to meet the supposed needs of some ruling group. Because Catholics obediently assume that those governing the Church are to be trusted, most of us are unaware that the New Covenant distortion exists in our Dogmatic Constitution. I ask the reader to compare the New Covenant of Jeremiah, 31:31 with that of Lumen Gentium, Chapt II No. 9 and the deceit becomes undeniably and shamefully obvious. It aims to falsify God's saving project.

God's relationship with us is established by Christ's death sealing the New Covenant whereby every human being is saved solely by God's goodness. Divine relationship is built solely by God and not by the teaching as dogmas mere human precepts. God through Christ has unilaterally performed the New Covenant because men had proved to be untrustworthy. Our <u>Dogmatic Constitution On The Church</u> is proof of man's perfidy. Catholicism is now based on needless teachings and needless forgivings of those already okay with God. The Church, thus, attempts to change the terms of the Covenant of <u>Jer</u> 31:31, which Christ already performs perfectly. To more effectively fulfill the Church's mission, let us enter into the dialogue "hoped for" by Vatican II (<u>Infra</u> No. 37.) and avoid he litigation that I am reluctant to bring.

Yours open to dialogue,

_____

March 23, 2009

Dear Holy Father,

I am outraged over the way the cult of ethnicity in the Church of Christ flagrantly quoted the New Covenant in order to furnish Catholics a Christian identity, deceitfully abusing God's saving action in history (see Chapt II, No. 9, <u>Dogmatic Constitution on the Church</u>).

I also find the silence I receive from my spiritual leaders disconcerting. I would think I would be the villain of the correspondence if there was an exchange, since my diocesan bishop's letter of August 2007 (the only response I ever received) advised me that my analysis was in error, that I need to improve on my obedience in faith to Church teaching, and I ought to seek direction from a certain theologian priest who I know as a childhood classmate of one of my sons.

The Inquisition once pursued heretics, but I am allowed to continue writing, receiving Holy Communion, and be both a lecturer and a Eucharistic minister. Yet, I remain ignorant of why my concerns are not of concern to my spiritual leaders. Your oppression blatantly violates my rights, vested in our <u>Dogmatic Constitution</u>, part No. 37. Still, I enjoy serving Christ.

I realize and appreciate that a dialogue with my pastor, the young priest who Bishop Wiegand referred me to, or anyone who cannot persuade you to change the ways of the Catholic Church is an act of futility and would be a painful experience for the priests. My diocesan bishop, Bishop Jaime Soto, might be one persuaded to amend the <u>Diocesan Statutes of the Third Diocesan Synod</u> (2006), but not if he has Bishop Wiegand's prejudices. I would willingly discuss those issues with him and all his theologians if he wishes and if there existed a hope to strike the Statutes down.

However, I believe my Holy Father Pope Benedict XVI, who I hardly know except by his writings, is solely responsible for the continuing absence of the fundamental virtue of charity expressed in both the Diocesan Statutes and the <u>Dogmatic Constitution on the Church</u>. I put to you that St. Paul's warnings at 1 <u>Cor</u> 11:29 applies to anyone who prevents a person from eating and drinking Christ's flesh "without recognizing the body" as an inclusion of every human being, thus bringing "a judgment on himself." Discriminating against sinners, or anyone whose evildoing God forgives, is uncharitable and a mortal sin of an anti-Christ blasphemy against the New Covenant.

You might argue the point with me. Correct me or be corrected in preparation for arguing with Jesus Christ at our judgment for messing with His gift to everyone.

Anxiously yours,

_____

March 25, 2009

Dear Holy Father,

Sunday, the Fourth Sunday of Lent, I was lecturer. Like the Persian Cyrus, I may have been inspired to proclaim the words of the Lord spoken by Jeremiah. The second reading that I read: God brought us to life with Christ, ". . . by grace you have been saved . . . and this is not from you, it is the gift of God; it is not from works . . ." (Ephesians 2:8–10). Earlier, the letter indicates that God, through Christ, destined us to be sons before the world began. This is what I write to you in my letters: that everyone created is Christ's siblings.

I suffered hearing this in the "Gospel Acclamation" and repeated in the Gospel According to John, "God so loved the world that he gave his only Son, so everyone who believes in him might have eternal life." If you read my letters, you would know why the underlined text bothers me. The author(s) of the Gospel knew the letter to the Ephesians, and they knew of St. Paul's claim that he heard from the Lord the words, "This cup is the new covenant in my blood" (1 Cor 11:25). They also knew of the Ephesians' letter accepting God's pledges to Jeremiah to teach and forgive us all in the Blood of the Covenant (see Eph 2). But, Iranaeus gave John's Gospel top-billing and Paul an unmentioned standing, even though his bias for John converting Polycarp overcame doubts that John authored the Fourth Gospel. We know Paul's message is from the Lord.

His Holiness Pope John XXIII and his assembled bishops in Council tried ressourcement to Christ's interdependent words and crucifixion, the source presumably of our New Covenant and Eucharist. A fruit of Vatican II was the theologians and the New Testament scholars' contention that Christ, in redeeming the world, meant for the Eucharistic sacrifices to be attended by all people of the worlds, not good Catholics alone. You personally preached and lectured that the New Covenant was that spelled out in Jeremiah. Jesus knew God's promised pledges by heart in Jer 31:31–34, and He died to establish them. It certainly was not the illegitimate offspring of the Catholic hierarchy spelled out in Lumen Gentium Chapt. II, No. 9.

The Associated Press quotes your advice in Angola for the war-ravaged continent—reconciliation calls for a "change of heart, a new way of thinking." I suggest you practice what you preach on return to Rome and invite everyone to Holy Communion. It is a reconciliation of which calls for you to have a "change of heart, a new way of thinking," more like that of Jesus Christ.

Yours open to dialogue,

———————————————

March 27, 2009

Dear Holy Father,

Two letters were erroneously mailed you on the 20th, revealing my fallibility. It evidences our equality to err, and it tends to prove undeniable that we are all created equal. As the fact becomes more commonly accepted in the world, people ask to be governed by those concerned with their equal rights. Democracy is winning in world politics, as His Holiness Pope Pius XII prophesied. God's people in the world show their popular choice for being governed by those who serve them impartially and not rule over them. Reinhold Neibuhr's Christian democracy rested on what God imprinted in man, "Man's capacity for justice makes democracy possible; man's inclination toward injustice makes democracy necessary." Neibuhr's New Covenant natures, and Christ's order to serve and not rule, should serve toward basis for Church democracy.

Since persuaded by St. Augustine's reading of Plato, the Roman Catholic Church, however, favors its own version of the Covenant—governing by an oligarchy. Thus, it favored fascism when Franco, Mussolini, and Hitler stripped the Basques in Spain of their democracy. Fascism was thought to be a bulwark against communism until Stalin won Hitler's war. Communism then opposed democracy and the Church during the Cold War. Russia folded a decade ago, and capitalism has progressed in China to bode well for democracy's struggle against totalitarianism. However, our Church's permanent government, convinced it rules by divine right, resists change and non-democratically persists as popes come and go. Pope John XXIII restrained the Curia in Vatican II, but he died in 1963. The reinstated bureaucracy continues to dilute, obstruct, and resist changes.

His Holiness Pope John XXIII and the world's assembled bishops of Vatican II established that the Church of Christ subsists in the Catholic Church over the traditionalists' argument for centuries that the Churches are identical. The New Testament scholars "tempted" you with the open Church's Eucharist, wherein Christ's covenanted people all share. But you asserted your own biased opinion of scripture to contradict the experts, and you argued St. Paul's letter to Corinth as a basis to exclude all those you deemed unworthily reconciled. Thereby, you unlovingly excommunicated most of humanity to their loss of Christ's actual presence (God Is Near Us, page 59), because you misinterpreted the New Covenant's scope and misread St. Paul's letter to the Corinthians.

In citing St. Paul in support of your opinion, you avoid his mention, in the same message he received from the Lord, "This cup is the new covenant in my blood" (1 Cor 11:25). You overlooked the words "New Covenant" that you preached were words interdependent with the death that redeemed the world (God Is Near Us, p. 29). Your selective word, "unworthily," also expands in meaning to justify humans excommunicating humans, rather than Christ later judging them. My Diocesan Statutes are a fruit of your opinion, as are the precepts of Ch. II, No. 9 of our Dogmatic Constitution. Both dare hold unclean those whom God purifies (Acts 10:15).

Yours open to dialogue,

———————————

Dear Holy Father,

Last Tuesday's introduction to my <u>Weekday Missal</u> stated, "Christ restores us to eternal life with God. This life comes through the Church and the sacraments. Baptism gives us supernatural life. The confessional brings the medicine to keep us alive. The Blessed Eucharist gives us strength. Left to ourselves, we have but a short cycle of life from birth to death. But through Christ and his Church we have the promise of life forever."

As a cradle Catholic, I was conditioned to believe just as the quotation above teaches. No wonder God provided in the New Covenant, ". . . I will place my law within them, and write it upon their hearts . . . No longer will they have need to teach their friends and kinsmen how to know the Lord. All, from least to greatest, shall know me, says the Lord, for I will forgive their evildoing and remember their sin no more." Note: no teacher need apply. God's saving and teaching action needs no Church indoctrination, as they probably would get it wrong.

Jesus Christ died to ratify and institute God's New Covenant relationship with every created human being, restoring life forever. This eternal life comes solely through Christ's performance of God's pledges. The Blessed Eucharist is part of Christ's gift, and the Church is merely a means of serving the Eucharistic sacrifice. Everyone created by God in his image is recreated from natural to supernatural beings solely by the efforts of Our Lord.

However, before God forgets our "sin," Jesus Christ may judge us all and chastise some for a time before we all are deemed perfect to share eternal life forever. Toward this aspect of our eternal lives, our faith and works, the Church and sacraments, play a part. In the Church, baptism enlivens us to be better, although, from conception, Christ already gives us supernatural life. Confession allows reconciliation to sustain our goodness, and it may affect the residuals of sin to lessen chastisement, not to affect our already secured gift of supernatural life.

Christ, not the Church, unconditionally graces the Blessed Sacrament, like redemption, to all humankind. Post Vatican II, the New Testament scholars tried to enlighten the Catholic Church on the inclusive Eucharist. Tragically, Joseph Ratzinger—as priest, bishop, and pope— failed to perceive the truth, and he enticed the Catholic Church to remain untrue to Christ, denying the Sacrament as did Donatism in St. Augustine's time.

I write to fulfill a Christian duty that says we lay Catholics have to express opinions on those things which concern the good of the Church (see ftnt #7 of No. 37, Chapt IV, <u>Lumen Gentium</u>). But, I am totally ignored. Why?

Yours open to dialogue,

April 1, 2009

Dear Holy Father,

You suggest that the real motive for lifting the excommunication of the four traditionalist bishops has nothing to do with Catholic relations to those outside the Church, but rather with healing the only formal schism within the Catholic Church in the last 100 years. Not reading my letters allows you to more comfortably say this historical fiction. I claim that a schism practiced for centuries is our Church's exclusive Eucharist based on the unworthiness of recipients. It is a schism because it fails to acknowledge Jesus' death as the fulfillment of God's New Covenant, which graced everyone with the worthiness to receive Christ's Presence.

We refuse to bear witness to Christ's New Covenant, and we do not hear Christ's words securing this covenantal relationship for us. Thus, the Catholic Church darkens our understanding of Christ. It blurs the spiritual faculties God imprinted in even the least of us. It deprives us of true faith. Christ suffered and died so that God's new relationship forgives our evildoings. Christ's cleansing includes those four traditional bishops, even Williamson, who continues to deny the Holocaust. So, your initial excommunication of them was null and void. We all, including all others the Church excommunicates, should learn more of the depth of God's love by devout sharing of the Eucharist and possessing Christ's passionate presence, transforming us into loving each other as equals.

Each Sacrifice of the Eucharist presumably has us all at the foot of the cross with Jesus freely offering himself up for us. We bless Christ for volunteering his excruciating death and for the fact he redeems the world. We experience Christ's death and God's covenantal forgiving by ingesting Holy Communion. He teaches and loves us while we unworthily live our lives of sin and receive His presence.

Please have your hierarchy restudy God's covenant, which Christ made in solidarity with all humanity. The gnats Jesus said we squeeze out are exemplified in the exclusive Church's Eucharist while it distributes to too few the Heavenly Nourishment Christ left to the whole world to transform everyone's life and faith. The Catholic Church's practice nullifies God's way of saving mankind. Worse, it substitutes in the Catholic way, which excommunicates even the more traditionalist of us as shown above. St. Paul warned those in Corinth that their discrimination uncharitably denied the "body" of Christ equal rights. Similar criticism applies to our exclusive Holy Communion and should bring judgment on us from Our Lord.

Today, in the USA, we have April Fool's Day. I wonder about my foolishness in writing you so much and so often, but I moreso question the wisdom of any who refuses to pay heed to Christ's teachings concerning His shedding of His Blood of the Covenant to establish the new relationship of God spelled out so plainly in His provisions and pledges.

Yours open to dialogue,

April 3, 2009

Dear Holy Father,

Jesus Christ gave a totally free gift to every created human being, a gift withheld from most of mankind by church religions. I speak of the gift of the Eucharist, which Jesus, likely speaking as instructed, gave us the night he was betrayed and immediately before being crucified. In anticipation of his death, he took bread, thanked God, broke it, and gave it to his disciples saying:

> Take this, all of you, and eat it: This is my body which will be given up for you.

Then he took a cup of wine, gave thanks and praise to God, and gave it to his disciples, saying:

> Take this, all of you, and drink from it: this is the cup of my blood, the blood of the <u>new and everlasting covenant</u>. It will be shed for you and for all so that sins may be forgiven. Do this in memory of me. (Emphasis mine)

To assure that humanity would get the message, the Glorified Jesus personally handed it on to learned Paul, repeating the words, "This is my body which is for you. Do this in remembrance of me," and, "This cup is the new covenant in my blood. Do this, whenever you drink it, in remembrance of me." Thus, the Eucharist was passed on to the Gentiles in Corinth and expectantly, in time, to everyone in the world.

But after two millenniums of withholding the Eucharist for Christians alone, post Vatican II scholars of the New Testament had to remind us that Christ meant for it to be unconditionally distributed to every human being. You recorded the New Testament scholars' efforts to do it Christ's way (<u>God Is Near Us</u>, page 59). Christ teaches that the purpose of the Eucharist is consumption by everyone as a means of teaching people about God with the real presence of Christ in the form of bread and wine. Thus, it is to nourish them, transforming their minds and hearts toward Jesus Christ. To make God's point, Jesus volunteered to excruciatingly die and intimately love us in his Eucharist. However, you contradicted the Bible experts with your own biased opinion.

Is it not long past time to join Jesus Christ in his efforts of relating God to everyone?

Yours persistently professing,

———————————————

April 6, 2009

Dear Holy Father,

Last April, at the UN General Assembly, you preached that they were obligated to uphold human rights, and you referred to the teachings of His Holiness Pope John XXIII. You and Pope John taught us that our failure to protect against violations of human rights makes governing bodies illegitimate.

It follows that the governing body of the Roman Catholic Church is illegitimate in that it denies redemption by Jesus Christ, a God-given right, to all but their destined believers in Christ. Yet, we should hold these truths to be undeniable—that all mankind was created equal; all were recreated equal in the Blood of the Covenant. To every right that God vested in us, everyone else owes a correlative duty. You spoke this truth correctly to the UN, while the governing body of the Catholic Church negates God's law of impartial love. We practice what Jesus said of paying him lip service while our hearts are far from him (<u>Mk</u> 7:6). Our dogma teaches only believers are redeemed and worthy of receiving the Eucharist.

I plan to publish a sequel to my book, <u>God's Gift To You</u> (2007). I will copy up to date messages of my concern, as well as all the letters that I dutifully mailed in expectation of the response of fatherly love which <u>Lumen Gentium</u> (Chapt IV, No. 37) promised me. Instead, I wish that you would apologetically respond to everyone in the world by distributing God's gift of love and teaching that it is for everyone's benefit.

Since mid-April 2008, I have again mailed you letters expressing my opinions for the Church on these matters of concern. Some earlier ones were hand-delivered to either Father Federico of your office or through my granddaughter Christina to Sister Palmara, who also assured her you would receive them, because her sisters made certain every letter sent to you was answered. Both Federico and Palmara may have delivered, but you never responded to me, violating of my rights by our <u>Dogmatic Constitution On The Church</u> (No. 37).

My spiritual leaders were obligated to consider my concerns with fatherly advice. The suggestions were meant to more effectively fulfill the Church's mission for life of the world. Now that I have been ignored, the Bible reads that I should refer my concerns for "Fraternal Correction" to the church (<u>Mt</u> 18:17). Those mainly harmed make up that part of the Church of Christ which does not subsist in the Catholic Church, to wit, all the rest of humanity. These many are denied the New Covenant rights so dearly gained them by Christ. We must return these vested rights to them and legitimize the mission of Catholicism to do charity for everyone. The Church of Christ subsists in the Catholic Church, but not wholly, yet.

I "telegraph my punch" so that whoever reads this letter might protect my Catholic Church from the scandal the disclosures may bring. The referral of my concerns to the world at large is in hopes someone will accomplish what you know you should do. I must proceed because I know not what else to do for Christ's sake and to salvage God's saving action in history. All those denied the Eucharist have vested rights in the Gift of God, and we have a correlative duty to deliver the Eucharist unconditionally.

Yours open to debate,

April 8, 2009

Dear Holy Father,

In my published book of letters to you, I invited all of the members of the Church of Christ, all our brothers and sisters in Christ, to join us in the Lord's Supper. In Christ, they are baptized in the Blood of the Covenant and make up the "body" with who we are to indiscriminately receive Holy Communion. I doubt if many of the "body" in the world would appreciate the story of the homeless women who confronted the Communion line in an inner-city church, followed the congregation, held out her hand, and to whom the priest unhesitantly said, "The Body of Christ." She consumed what she received and interiorly possessed the Real Presence of God (God's Gift To You, page 51). The minister may have recognized the "body" in the homeless person, as we should also see Christ in everyone, but Our Lord appreciated the chance to transform her life.

I doubt if you read the book or any letter I wrote before or after publication. I am publishing a sequel simply to record all my letters concerning the "body," the unrecognized global Church of Christ. Someday, someone will awaken from the darkness to which our hierarchy and traditions have left us in. Presumably, the Holy Spirit oversees the Church, but does not interfere. The Catholic Church's clinging to traditions of exclusion of so many from our Eucharist obviously lacks the love of our neighbors that Christ desires. I think it is done without recognizing the "body" (1 Cor 11:29). Not recognizing the "body" is an evildoing—forgiven, although not forgotten. We await judgment of Jesus Christ on our conduct. I pray that the chastisement we merit will be short. Likely, at your and my respective ages, we will soon know the judgment we brought on ourselves because of maintaining our Church's Eucharist, excluding so many from the Sacrament. It makes for a Church untrue to the Church of Christ.

I want you to know that I enjoyed expressing my opinions concerning the good of the Church and its fulfillment of its mission for the life of the world. In trying different ways to gain your attention, I learned so much of Our Lord and me. However, what I experienced best was participating in our Eucharist sacrifice. My reflections on Jesus Christ's moments nailed to that cross and excruciatingly persevering to do what he thought he ought to do to satisfy His Father personally established our covenant relationship. His failure to conform the Catholic Church to the Church of Christ, and my total inability to reach my spiritual leaders' hearts or minds with my written concerns, made me thankful to Our Lord for allowing me to have in common the effort to do the will of God for everyone, even though I proved so inept.

Being ineffective shames me, as does being a Catholic whose Church excommunicates most people from receiving the same gift that I enjoy, even though God vested in each and every one of us our right to the gift with no strings attached. Not only do we not recognize the "body," but God too is shorted of the love and thanks from so many excluded from our Eucharist. God is entitled to have us retain the Eucharist's saving action and thanksgiving in the Church of Christ. In exchange for God's gift and unilateral performance of the New Covenant, simply out of His loving goodness, He is entitled at least to everyone's thanks.

Yours open to dialogue,

_____

Dear Holy Father,

Due to mini-strokes that I am likely sustaining, I cannot read what I write, forcing me to cease corresponding attempts. Someone may say it is long past time to terminate my monologue. One or both of us may have much tried Christ's patience.

Coincidently, as lecturer my last Epistle reading was the New Covenant (Jer 31:31 *ff*). The reading and this ailment possibly tell me "enough is enough." This morning I could not read the Entrance Antiphon, "Christ is the mediator of a new covenant so that, since he has died, those who are called may receive the eternal inheritance promised to them" (Heb 9:15), or the Communion Antiphon, which read "God did not spare his own Son, but gives him up for us all with Christ he will surely give us all things" (Rom 8:32) (Emphasis mine). Apparently, Christ still teaches us that his testamentary bequest continues to benefit everyone.

As I write off my concerns for the good of the Church, I leave you with the warning that you should be concerned for your personal record. In the future, some of us may conclude that you "sold your soul," as we say, to attain your present title. If true, in not recognizing the body of Christ, you are asking for Christ's judgment. My letters hint at this possibility, but you can dispel any worry if you change your heart. Your delay, however, may assure sterner chastisement and be interpreted as an admission of willful wrongdoing.

You surely have time and opportunity to correct the exclusiveness of the Church's Eucharist, and, more importantly, correct the negation of God's saving way that detours us into distorting our recognition of the true Covenant in "Light of Nations" (Ch. II, No. 9). It reveals our misunderstanding of Christ's purpose and the New Covenant relationship that Christ established between God and every created human being, assuring peace based on everyone's salvation.

A start would be to invite everyone, regardless of their state or condition of sinfulness, to our Church's Eucharist. The invitation obeys what Jesus ordered in Jerusalem two millenniums ago. The delayed compliance should be explained, similar to repenting, as due to our fallible translating of what Jesus and God provided for our salvation in history. Should you miss this opportunity, I prophesize that, in time, humanity will evolve to correct enlightenment, taking and consuming the Holy Communion together and in obedience to Jesus Christ. We cannot wait on the Catholic Church to awaken to the fact that its negation of God's saving action in history is anti-Christ. "Awake, O sleeper . . . and Christ will give you light."

Anyway, God brings good out of all our wrongdoings or humanness. Whatever we leave amiss, God will make good here or hereafter, and we will all end up happy with Jesus Christ and Our Creator Lord regardless, as was intended from the beginning. I say this, trusting it is from on-High, from the heart.

Farewell,

Printed in the United States
by Baker & Taylor Publisher Services